SewBasic

SewBasic

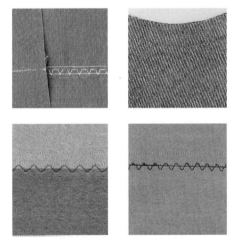

34 Essential Skills
for Sewing with
Confidence

From the editors of THREADS magazine

The Taunton Press

The Taunton Press, Inc., 63 South Main Street, PO Box 5506, Newtown, CT 06470-5506

The Taunton Press
Inspiration for hands-on living™

e-mail: tp@taunton.com

Distributed by Publishers Group West

JACKET/COVER DESIGNER: MARY MCKEON
INTERIOR DESIGNER: SUSAN FAZEKAS
LAYOUT ARTIST: SUSAN FAZEKAS
FRONT COVER PHOTOGRAPHER: JACK DEUTSCH, © JACK DEUTSCH
BACK COVER PHOTOGRAPHER: SLOAN HOWARD, © SLOAN HOWARD

LIBRARY OF CONGRESS CATALOGING-IN-PUBLICATION DATA
Sew basic : 34 essential skills for sewing with confidence / [the editors of Threads].
      p. cm.
    Includes bibliographical references and index.
    ISBN 1-56158-541-6
      1. Sewing. 2. Dressmaking. I. Threads (Newtown, Conn.)

TT705 .S453 2002
646.2–dc21   2001057378

Printed in the United States of America
10 9 8 7 6 5 4 3 2

The following manufacturers/names appearing in *SewBasic* are registered trademarks or servicemarks: 3M, Bernina, Do-Sew, Fiskars, Gingher, Lycra, Pellon, Pfaff, Polarfleece, Scotch, Teflon, Ultrasuede.

132,017
£12.72

Acknowledgments

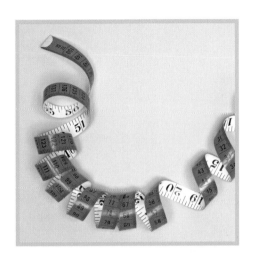

Special thanks to the editors, art directors, copy editors, and other staff members of Threads who contributed to the development of the articles featured in this book.

Contents

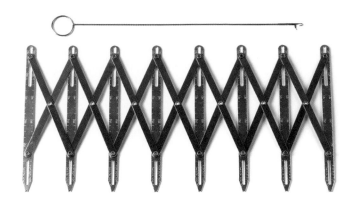

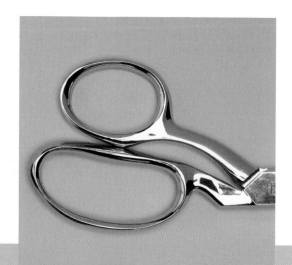

Introduction

have you always wanted to sew but felt you simply didn't know where to begin? Or has it been years since you used your sewing machine for anything other than mending, and now you can't remember how to read a pattern, much less how to sew in a zipper or create pleats? Relax.

Sewing is not a mysterious art requiring great innate talent. It's a skill, and like any skill, it can be learned and enjoyed by nearly anyone. All that's required are a bit of eye-hand coordination, the ability to think logically as you follow directions, and the understanding of some basic sewing terms. To help you hone these skills is a collection of 34 articles from *Threads* magazine that will give you the confidence to sew nearly any project you want to undertake.

Confidence begins with feeling comfortable buying a pattern and the right fabric and supplies you need for a project and ends with a garment that looks every bit as perfect as if a professional had made it. With the basic skills included in *SewBasic* you can sew that perfect garment and it will fit and look better than any mass-produced garment you could buy in a department store. So, what are you waiting for? Get sewing! ▪

First things first.

Experienced sewers will tell you that a carefully prepared project goes together much easier, so in this section we explain what you need to do to get started on the right foot. From shopping for fabric and notions through choosing and fitting a pattern all the way to cutting out and marking your fabric, the steps you need to take before you sew are clearly explained. And if you want to make home accessories rather than garments, you can skip the pattern-fitting steps. You'll find the rest of the information just as useful, whether you're sewing a dress or a slipcover or curtains. ■

part 1

Before You Sew

A Trip to the Fabric Store

for most sewers, a trip to the fabric store is a little bit of heaven. But if you're a beginner, this experience might be somewhat overwhelming. So many choices. But there's no one way to approach shopping—sometimes you'll choose a pattern first, then the fabric, or just the opposite. At times you might even start with a button or trim. Here are some tips to help you narrow down your options when you select a pattern, to get the proper fabric yardage amounts, and to find the notions for your project.

The innumerable offerings at the fabric store need not overwhelm. To make shopping easier, get familiar with the information on pattern envelopes, check the facts about a fabric on the bolt or tag, and match notions when purchasing fabric.

Buying a Pattern

Most pattern companies organize their catalogs according to type of garment, but many separates can be found in other categories. With time, you'll get to learn each company's way of naming and grouping their patterns.

When you've found a pattern you like, ask the sales clerk to get it for you or, if it is permitted, find it yourself. Patterns are usually grouped by manufacturer and arranged in drawers, in numerical order with usually at least one of each size available—the size is usually printed at the top of the pattern envelope. On the envelope you'll find recommendations for types and amounts of fabric and a list of notions and other supplies, such as interfacing, lining, and trims needed for the project. Some pattern companies indicate the degree of difficulty on the envelope,

but for other patterns, you might need to read the instructions to see how complex the construction looks. (You don't have to buy the pattern to do this.) That way you'll be sure it's a pattern with which you and your sewing skills are comfortable.

Fabric-Buying Tips

Fabrics are seasonal, just like ready-to-wear. Information about each fabric is usually printed at the top of each bolt or on a separate tag. It should include fiber content, fabric width, and price per yard. Yardage requirements for the garment you want to make are listed on the pattern envelope according to fabric width, most commonly

45 in. and 60 in. but also in 36-in., 48-in., and 54-in. widths.

Often you look at a fabric and immediately it "just hits you" what you want to do with it—the specific design may take a while to come. If you see a fabric you love but just can't make a decision, most fabric stores are happy to cut a little swatch for you to take home and consider what you want to make with it. But don't wait too long because this fabric may not be available later. You may want to get the maximum amount for a garment you most likely will make with the fabric (look at two or three patterns to give you an idea). You can always use leftover fabric for bindings, quilting, scarves, or sachets.

Going for Extra Yardage

Some pattern pieces may not fit economically on 36-in.-wide fabric, so it's best to check the pattern layouts on the instruction sheet to see if there is one already plotted for this width. If there isn't one, you may have to ask a sales clerk for help in not only buying extra fabric but also in how the pieces should be laid out—you may have to work with reversing pattern pieces on a single layer of fabric, and that takes careful planning. If you already own the pattern, you can pull out the pattern pieces themselves to see if you can lay them out on 36-in.-wide fabric.

Otherwise, you will have to buy the pattern and then work out the fabric amount.

Cutting layouts are now generated by computer, so suggested yardage amounts are pretty accurate. But if you need to alter your pattern by adding or subtracting length or width, you may need more or less fabric than the yardage suggested. When adding length, a good rule is to multiply the amount added by the number of garment pieces affected. You can find finished garment lengths on the instruction sheet or the envelope to help you determine changes. (Be sure to make the same changes for interfacing and lining amounts as well.)

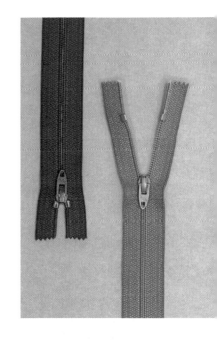

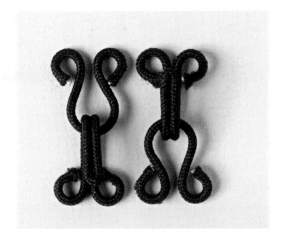

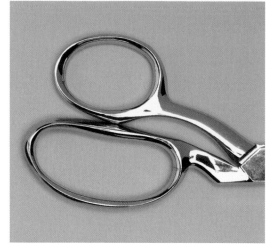

Fabric Substitution

Most patterns are designed with specific fabrics in mind. You can substitute from the recommended list, but it's best if you stay with a fabric that's similar in weight and drape. And if a pattern is designed for knit fabrics only, using a woven fabric instead will mean that you'll have to alter the amount of ease in the garment in order to allow for body movement.

Notions and Other Supplies

Depending on the garment, you may also need thread, a zipper, buttons, trim, inter-

facing, and lining fabric. The pattern envelope will list the specifics, but if you haven't chosen a pattern, it's a good idea to buy one or two spools of matching thread at the time you purchase your fabric. If you can't find an exact match, choose thread that's a shade darker because it will blend in better and be less noticeable than a lighter shade.

Zippers are available in limited colors, so if you can't find an exact match, again choose a slightly darker shade or a color that blends well with your fabric. You'll also need to choose the correct zipper length, which will be given on the pattern envelope, but if you don't have a pattern in mind, use a 7-in. or 9-in. zipper for skirts and pants and an 18 in.- to 22-in. one for the back opening on a dress.

The number and size of buttons needed are also given on the pattern, but the style and type of button is up to you. If you can't find a button that's exactly the color you want, consider using a covered button. Many fabric stores have a service to professionally cover buttons in various styles and sizes if you provide a piece of your fabric. If you're making a special trip to the fabric store for notions, be sure to carry along swatches of your fabrics to help with matching. ■

Grainline

grain, or grainline, refers to the orientation of the yarns in woven fabric. The warp yarns run from back to front in the weaving loom and form the lengthwise grain—often called the straight grain. The weft yarns are woven from side to side into the warp yarns and form the crosswise grain, or crossgrain. The lengthwise and crosswise grains are perpendicular to one another in the loom. The bias falls along any angle to the lengthwise or crosswise grain, (see the drawing below) and the true bias is at a 45-degree angle to the straight grain. Non-woven fabrics, such as felts, have no grain.

How the Grainlines Behave

Since the warp yarns are tightly stretched during the weaving process, the lengthwise grain has very little, if any, give, or stretch. Most garments are cut with the lengthwise grain oriented vertically, perpendicular to the hem, because the warp yarns hold their shape well and resist bagging and stretching. See the photos on p. 11, which compare the drape of fabric on its different grains. This

Fabric Grain

Grain refers to the orientation of the yarns in a woven fabric. Warp yarns, parallel to the selvage, form the lengthwise grain. Weft yarns, perpendicular to the selvage, form the crossgrain. Bias refers to any line that falls at a diagonal angle to the selvage. True bias falls at a 45-degree angle.

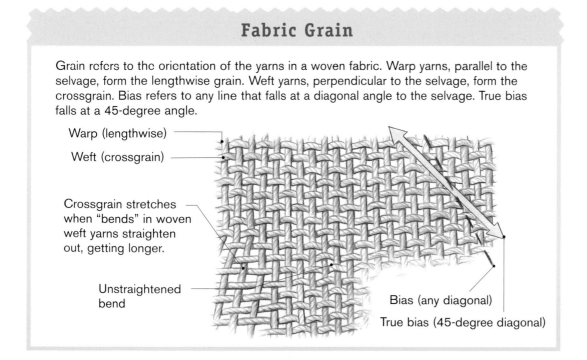

Warp (lengthwise)

Weft (crossgrain)

Crossgrain stretches when "bends" in woven weft yarns straighten out, getting longer.

Unstraightened bend

Bias (any diagonal)

True bias (45-degree diagonal)

Straightening Grain

Checking for Square

STEP 1. Determine cross-grain by pulling crossgrain thread.

STEP 2. Cut along pulled thread line to mark cross-grain.

STEP 3. Fold fabric length-wise, smoothing fold and aligning selvages. Fabric is off grain if the layers are not aligned across each end.

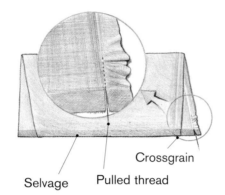

Selvage

Crossgrain

Pulled thread

Restoring Square

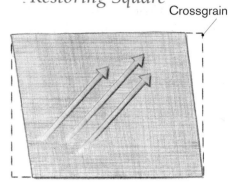

Crossgrain

Hold the fabric at opposite diagonal corners and pull gently. Be sure to hold and pull in the direction opposite to the direction of distortion.

places the crossgrain, which has greater stretch, horizontally around the body, allowing the fabric to ease as the yarns flex with the body's movement (see the bottom left section of the drawing on p. 9). The crossgrain is rarely placed vertically in a garment because it will droop as the yarns relax.

Because fabric cut on the bias distorts and stretches (with the maximum stretch along the true bias), it drapes beautifully over the body's contours. Designers often use the characteristic drape of a bias cut to create dramatic clinging effects in their garments. Because of the stretch and distortion of the bias, garment pieces cut on the bias need special handling during cutting and construction. While bias-cut garments require a little extra effort to construct, the rewards are considerable in terms of drape and play of fabric patterns.

Checking for Square

Once a fabric has been woven, it can be pulled out of square, or off grain, during other manufacturing steps, such as when it's folded and rolled onto bolts. When the fab-

ric is off grain, the warp and weft yarns are no longer at right angles to one another. If the grain is not straightened before cutting, the garment will likely fit strangely or hang crookedly.

To determine if fabric is off grain, nick the selvage with scissors near one end of the fabric length. Then grasp one or two crossgrain threads, and pull them gently, as shown in the left-hand drawing above. Cut the end of the fabric along the line created by the pulled thread. Then, with the fabric lying smoothly on your worktable, fold the fabric in half lengthwise, aligning the selvage edges. If the two layers of the cut end (the crossgrain) do not line up, the fabric is off grain. You can also use an L-square to check the alignment; just position the corner of the square at the cut end of the fabric with one leg of the square along the selvage. The cut end of the fabric should align with the other leg of the square.

Squaring the grainlines

If the fabric is off grain, you can often restore the perpendicular alignment of the length-wise and crosswise yarns; this process is called squaring or, somewhat illogically, straightening. Some fabric finishes seem to resist squaring. Prewashing a washable fabric will soften the yarns and make them easier to square, as will lightly steaming the fabric.

Square the alignment by holding the fabric at opposite diagonal corners and pulling gently (see the drawing at right on p. 10). Be sure to hold and pull in the direction opposite to the direction of distortion—the idea is to work the yarns back into square, not pull them further out. Then refold the fabric to see if the crossgrain is square with the lengthwise grain. If not, gently pull the fabric on the diagonal again. Continue these steps until the fabric is squared, then press the fabric in the direction of the lengthwise grain only. This method also works for realigning a knit that has been pulled off grain.

Commercial Pattern Grainlines

Because fabric behaves differently along its various grainlines, every commercial pattern piece is marked with the recommended grainline orientation so the garment will fit according to the designer's intentions. The arrow on each pattern piece, which indicates the lengthwise grain, should be placed on the fabric parallel to the selvage. Even small pieces such as collars, cuffs, and facings work best when oriented on the recommended grainline.

But pattern pieces for some garments, such as gored skirts, can be cut with the arrow on the bias in order to increase drape and make interesting use of stripes and other fabric motifs. If you want to do this, mark a new straight grainline on the pattern piece at a 45-degree angle to the printed arrow (use a 45-degree triangle). But plan carefully before cutting to be sure you understand the way the stripes will align from one pattern piece to the next—it's easy to get confused.

With the lengthwise grain perpendicular to the floor, this soft, fluid silk crepe maintains some body, with folds beginning toward the top of the dress form.

With the crossgrain perpendicular to the floor, the silk has a similar drape but less body. It will stretch and droop over time.

Silk crepe hung with the bias perpendicular to the floor molds to the dress form, revealing every contour underneath.

Knitted Fabrics

The orientation of the yarn in knitted fabrics is described by "direction" instead of grainline. Direction refers to the lengthwise ribs and crosswise courses. Unlike woven fabrics, knits have the greatest amount of stretch along the crosswise course; thus, a knit's bias direction has less stretch than its crosswise direction. Most often, garments made from knit fabric are cut with the lengthwise direction perpendicular to the hem. ■

Choose the Correct Pattern Size

the first step to making a garment that fits well is to choose the correct pattern size. This may seem obvious, but it's surprising how many sewers start with the wrong size, then end up making a lot of adjustments to get a good fit.

Measurements Are Key

When choosing a pattern size, you need to know some basic body measurements (see the measurement chart on the facing page) —you can't simply rely on your ready-to-wear size when it comes to choosing pat-terns. In this era of skinny models and movie stars, designers and manufacturers frequently use what's called "vanity sizing"— inches added to each size to attract a buyer to a label that tells her she's smaller than she really is! What might have been a size 16 a few years ago is labeled a size 10 or 12 today! With sizing so inconsistent, most of us fit into a wide range of sizes.

Among the major pattern companies, however, sizing is based on a standard set of body measurements, which are provided on each pattern envelope and at the back of the pattern catalogs. Once you've determined your pattern size by comparing your measurements with these standards, you can purchase that size for any of the company's patterns. But because very few figures will match a pattern company's standard measurements exactly, below are some guidelines for choosing a pattern size.

Comparing Measurements

First if you're unsure of which size category your body type fits into, such as misses', women's, or petite's, check your height and back-waist length measurements, and compare them to the measurement charts provided on the back of each pattern catalog. Then take your full-bust, high-bust, waist,

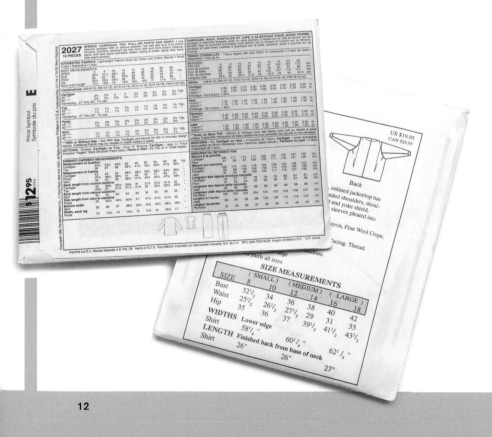

and hip measurements, and compare them with the standard measurements within that figure category.

When you choose a blouse, dress, or jacket pattern, compare your high-bust measurement with the standard bust measurement on the chart to get the best fit in the shoulder area. It's important to fit the shoulder area first because this area is harder to alter on a pattern than the bust cup, waist, and hip.

When choosing pants and skirt patterns, compare the waist and hip measurements: Your choice will be determined by your hip measurement. If the skirt is full, use your waist measurement to select a pattern size.

If your measurements fall between two sizes, consider your bone structure. If you're small-boned, buy the smaller size; conversely, if you're large-boned, buy the larger.

Consider Garment Ease

To fit comfortably, a garment must have ease built into it: Wearing ease is the minimum amount of inches added to a pattern so that you can move in the garment, and design ease is the amount the designer added or subtracted to create a particular silhouette. Ease allowances, found at the back of the pattern catalogs, may vary slightly from company to company and in some cases the ease allowed may affect the size pattern you choose. For example, if a style is loose-fitting with a large amount of ease and you prefer a closer fit, you might decide to choose a smaller size.

So get out a tape measure to find your correct size. In most cases, your pattern size will probably be larger than your ready-to-wear size, but when you start with the right number, fitting is so much easier. ■

Personal Measurement Chart

Take and record your basic body measurements wearing well-fitting undergarments. Tie ¼-in. elastic around your waist to find exact placement. Hold the tape measure snugly but not tightly.

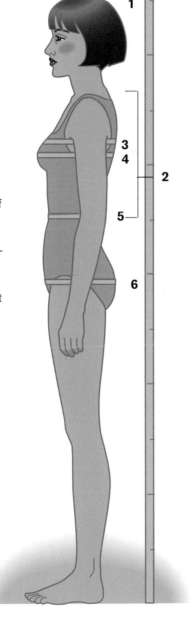

1. Height: Without shoes, standing against a wall

2. Back-waist length: From prominent bone at base of neck to natural waistline

3. High bust: High up under arms across chest and back

4. Full bust: Straight across back and around fullest part of bust

5. Waist: Around body at natural waistline

6. Hips: Around body at fullest part of hips

Making a Duplicate Pattern

most pattern collectors like to keep their patterns intact. Even if you don't plan on making adjustments to a pattern, down the road sometimes you do, so it helps to have a copy of the original to use as a reference or to reuse in another size. Tracing a pattern can be done quickly and accurately with a few simple steps and some basic tools. It is important to note, however, that patterns have copyrights. When you make a duplicate, remember that it should not be used for anything other than your personal sewing.

Tracing Tips

Before addressing the tools needed to trace, let's look at the tracing process. It may seem apparent, but the following guidelines will make tracing a pattern easy and accurate.

For fast, accurate tracing, use a ruler as a guide to trace grainlines and straight seamlines. Extend the grainlines to make it easier to align the pattern and fabric when cutting.

STEP 1. Start by taping the original pattern tissue to a table so it won't shift. Then place the tracing paper over the pattern and use tape or weights to hold it in place.

STEP 2. Using a long ruler, trace the marked grainline arrow or mark, extending it the length of the pattern piece if possible; this makes it easier to align the pattern and fabric. Use the ruler to trace all your vertical lines first. Then trace all horizontal lines and do your curves last. This is a more efficient use of the ruler and will speed up copying.

STEP 3. To make tracing curves easier, use a shorter ruler as a guide (or do it free-hand) and draw a series of dashes, about ¼ in. to ½ in. apart, along the curves.

STEP 4. Finally, trace the darts and any other internal markings. Write on each pattern section the pattern number, size, number of fabric pieces to cut, and amounts to allow for seams and hems.

Tracing Papers

In addition to many types of tracing paper available from art-supply and stationery stores, there are papers specifically designed for tracing patterns (see Resources on p. 87). A versatile, all-purpose white paper called Pattern Paper is similar to the paper used on medical examining tables and is easy to use and inexpensive. For a more transparent paper—useful when cutting out fabrics that need to be matched—try Do-Sew™ Tracing

Paper or Burda's Tracing Set, a plastic-like paper that comes with a marking pen.

Grid paper can be useful for aligning a pattern's straight edges and squared corners. Pellon® Tru Grid® is a drapable, nonwoven, interfacing-like paper that can be sewn and used to make a fitting shell as well as a pattern. This type of paper also clings to the fabric, making it easier to cut out fabrics that are slippery or have a lofty pile like Polarfleece™, which seems to resist pattern tissue. Burda also makes a gridded tissue paper.

Rulers, Markers, and Tracing Wheels

Use a ruler to help trace long, straight seamlines and grainlines. A flexible, transparent 3-in. by 18-in. ruler works well. When tracing curves, use a shorter 1-in. by 6-in. ruler.

Simple mechanical pencils or ballpoint pens are the best drawing tools because the lines will not vary in width. There is also a rolling felt marker on the market called Roll-a-Pattern, which makes tracing especially fast. You can use felt-tip markers, but be careful that they don't bleed or make too broad a line.

You may also want to try marking with a sharp pinpoint tracing wheel. Use this for tracing onto heavier paper like oaktag (similar to a file folder). Place the paper under the pattern and trace along the lines (be sure to protect your table). The needlelike points will mark the outline of the pattern piece, and you can highlight the lines later with pencil or pen.

Multiple Pattern Pieces

When the same pattern piece needs to be cut more than once from the fabric, make multiple copies of it. This makes laying out the pattern much easier, especially when the pattern layout is for a single layer of fabric.

To make a pair of copies, layer two pieces of tracing paper together before you trace,

Curves can be traced with a series of dashes, either freehand or using a short ruler as a guide.

and you can cut them both at the same time. When you are adding reference marks, darts, and so on, always be sure to indicate right and left sections on the appropriate sides of the copies.

There are times when you may want to make a whole pattern piece instead of the half pieces that are to be cut on the fabric's fold. To accomplish this, just trace the pattern section onto a folded piece of paper, cut, and open it out.

What about Photocopying?

This is a very fast way to produce a copy, but be careful because photocopying usually creates some distortion—it's best to use this process only for pattern pieces that will fit onto one sheet of paper (letter or legal size). Before you use it as a pattern piece, check each copy against the original to make sure it's been accurately reproduced. ■

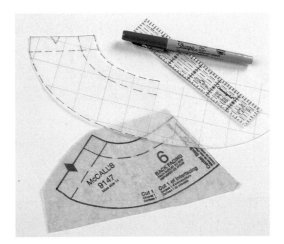

To create a whole pattern piece, trace a half-pattern to a folded piece of paper by placing the pattern's foldline on the paper's fold.

Tissue- and Pin-Fitting

no matter how expensive, clothing off the rack can't compare with custom-fit garments. To give you a great fit in clothes you sew, here are two professional techniques, tissue-fitting and pin-fitting. Both are good investments—whatever time and energy you spend on fitting will pay off in great sewing results!

Try On the Taped Tissue

If your body is fairly symmetrical, you can tissue-fit only one side and make needed changes.

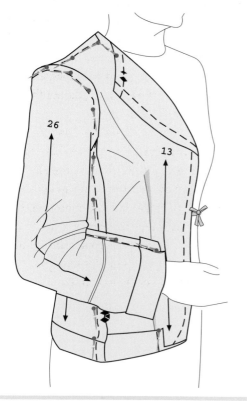

26

13

First, Tissue-Fit

In a nutshell, tissue-fitting involves pinning or taping the pressed pattern pieces together, trying on the paper half-garment, noting areas that need correcting, making fitting adjustments to the pattern, and then repeating the process until you're happy with it. If your body is fairly symmetrical, you can work with the half-pattern and adjust only one side (you'll cut both sides the same), but if you're noticeably different on each side, copy the pattern pieces so you have a full paper garment, and tissue-fit the sides individually.

STEP 1. Check the amount of ease. First, decide how much ease you want in your garment. It helps to compare the pattern with an old, trusted pattern or garment. Check the shoulder width, neckline, armhole depth, bustline, waist, hip, and length. If you know your figure irregularities, you can begin to adjust for them before you tissue-fit.

STEP 2. Prepare the pattern. Patterns without seam allowances, like Neue Mode and older Burda patterns, are easy to tape together and tissue-fit and will give very accurate results. For patterns with seam allowances, it's easiest to fold back one seam allowance (clipping the edge, if needed) and lap it over the second one, matching the seamlines. (Then reinforce the clipped area with tape or fusible interfacing when you're ready to cut out the garment.) Join pattern pieces as follows, using removable (blue label) Scotch™ tape, which can be positioned over and over—pins work also.

STEP 3. To assemble the "pattern garment," attach the bodice front and back at the sides and shoulders. If your pattern has a skirt, attach it to the bodice, matching seamlines. Pin the sleeve together, and attach the cuff, if any; don't attach the sleeve to the garment. Pin up the hemlines, then pin a length of seam tape or ribbon around the waistline of the pattern. On a close-fitting garment, put the ribbon on the outside; on a loose-fitting garment, pin the ribbon loosely to the inside to hold it at the waistline. If you plan to use a shoulder pad, pin it in place now.

STEP 4. Try on the tissue—it's great to have a helper to pin or tape the back, but you can still get good results working alone. Wearing the underwear and any clothing you'll wear beneath the finished garment, slip the tissue on your body and tie the ribbon around your waist. Pin or tape the pattern to your clothing at the neckline, bust, waist, and hip, in front and back. Slip the sleeve on and pin it to the bodice at match points in the front armhole and shoulder. A weighted drapery cord (available at shops selling drapery fabric) positioned around the neck helps establish a flattering and comfortable neckline, and you can pin through it.

STEP 5. Take a look! Evaluate your pattern in front of a full-length mirror, using a hand mirror to see the back. Since a pattern hangs from the shoulders, begin at the top and check the following points:

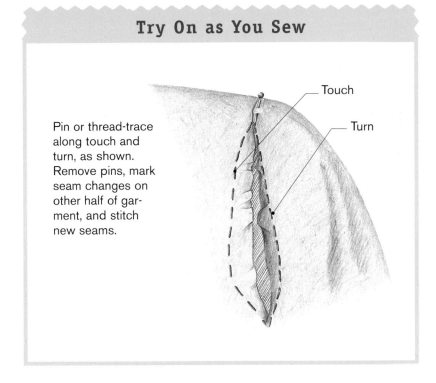

Try On as You Sew

Pin or thread-trace along touch and turn, as shown. Remove pins, mark seam changes on other half of garment, and stitch new seams.

Touch

Turn

a. The shoulder seam should lie on the top of the shoulder and end at the shoulder joint, so adjust as needed. Bust darts should point to the bust and end before its fullest point. Check to make sure the pattern tissue reaches the center front and center back. If it doesn't, let out the side seams.

b. Vertical seams should hang perpendicular to the floor. If they don't, adjust them at the shoulders or waist.

c. The sleeve should fit comfortably around the arm; check to be sure that any elbow shaping actually occurs at the elbow. Bend your arm to check the length—you can raise the cap of the sleeve, and many times raise the sleeve/bodice underarm seam to increase mobility. If there is too much cap, or if the underarm is too high, it's very easy to cut off the excess during assembly.

Working from right to left, pick up thread on back layer, insert needle in fold of front layer, and pull through to complete stitch. Repeat to end.

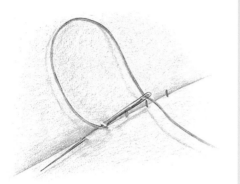

Slip-baste to mark.

d. The seam tape or ribbon around the waist makes it easy to check the bodice length. Lifting your shoulders without tearing the tissue ensures a comfortable amount of blousing.

Final Fine Points

Take the paper pattern off and make any necessary adjustments to it, then try the tissue on again and check the fit. When you're finally happy with the pattern, you're ready to cut the fabric, but be sure to leave generous seam allowances in the fitting seams (shoulder, side, waistline, and sleeve) for any additional adjustments you make as you sew.

Fine-tune with pin-fitting

- As you sew your garment, pin-fit to customize the fit. Your choice of fabric influences the fit, and one alteration may affect or correct another.

- As soon as you assemble the main pieces of the garment, try it on right side out and check the fit. Don't overfit—too close a fit

will accent any figure irregularity. Your garment should allow you to move comfortably.

- Some fine-tuning suggestions: You may want to curve the shoulder seams and bust and hip darts so that they fit the contours of your body. Check the ease in the bustline and the fit across the back and at the waistline.

- Check the hang of the sleeve and the fit of the cap area. For set-in sleeves, pin the sleeve into the garment before sewing, placing the top of the sleeve so the cross-grain line is parallel to the floor. Check to see that the sleeve hangs gracefully, and make sure that you can move your arms to the front and back comfortably.

Alter as You Pin-Fit

Since pin-fitting is done on the right side of the garment, you'll need to transfer changes accurately to the wrong side in order to incorporate them into your construction and blend the new seamline with the original one. A fast method of stitching a pin-fitted seamline is to slip-baste the seam as shown above, then flip the fabric layers so the seam allowance extends, and machine-stitch on the basted line. The drawback is that it's difficult to transfer changes to the other side of the garment or to the pattern.

For a marking method that's easy to transfer to the other side, use pins or thread tracing to mark both sides of the corrected seam, where the two fabric layers touch. After marking, remove the pins and mark the adjustment on the other side of the garment and on the tissue. Stitch the seams on the new seamlines. ■

Making Your Mark

transferring construction details from garment pattern to fabric is essential to a successful sewing project—perhaps second in importance only to laying out a pattern on the correct grainline! But, if you're like most (truthful) sewers, you may sometimes find marking time-consuming and difficult. The goal of marking is to transfer pattern marks accurately without damaging the fabric, and (if you're lucky) the process should be quick and easy.

For marks to work, they have to show on your fabric, last for as long as they're needed, and (very important) come out of the fabric when you want them to. The key to successful marking is using the right method for your fabric. Every fabric reacts differently to marking, so let's talk first about marking methods and materials, then look at how to match the method to the fabric.

Thread Marks Are Reliable

Traditional thread tracing and tailor's tacks take time, but they're reliable for marking any fabric. (See the drawings at right and on p. 20.) Because polyester thread can leave impressions or damage your fabric when pressed or pulled out, use either lightweight cotton or silk thread—for delicate fabrics, be sure to use silk thread.

You may find that half your thread marks wiggle out of the fabric and onto the floor

before you get to the construction step where they're needed, but a piece of Sewers Fix-it Tape (see Resources on p. 87; also available from medical-supply stores, sold as 3M™ Micropore tape) will hold them in place. Be sure to remove the tape in four to five days because its adhesive will leave a sticky residue if left on the fabric too long.

Thread Tracing

Through a Single Layer

Working on one fabric layer, transfer pattern marks to fabric with pins, then fold pattern back and pin it out of the way. Using silk or fine cotton thread, trace line with long and short stitches.

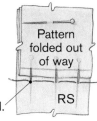

Pins mark line to be thread-traced.

Through Multiple Layers

1. Baste through all layers, leaving very long loops between stitches.

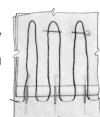

2. Separate layers without pulling loops taut, and clip threads between layers, then clip loops on pattern side, and hold threads in place while removing pattern.

Tape ends to prevents threads from falling out.

Traditional Tailor's Tacks

Slit pattern mark with needle point; then, with double strand of thread, take one small stitch through all layers, leaving long tails and loop.

Remove pattern piece, separate fabric layers, pulling threads taut, then clip.

Modified Tailor's Tacks on a Raw Edge

1.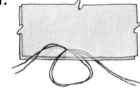

2.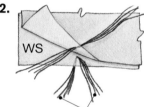

1. With double strand of thread, stitch through all layers ¼ in. from raw edge, leaving long tails and large loop.

2. Separate layers and clip loop. Hold thread tails together with glue stick.

3.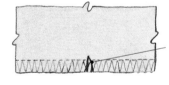

3. Serge or machine-stitch edge finish.

Stitching holds threads in place.

Harder Isn't Better: Scissor and Pins

There was a time when a marking method was good only if it was painstaking. Nowadays sewers go for what's fast and easy, provided it works. A scissors' snip in the seam allowance is the quickest way to transfer notches and seamline marks to a nonravelly fabric when the seam (like that inside a waistband) will be edge-finished or buried. Snip the raw edge (no more than ¼ in. for a ⅝-in. seam allowance) perpendicular to the seamline, which helps to correctly match the corresponding points on two garment pieces. In addition to marking seamline details, a cut can be used in seam allowances to mark foldlines.

Using pins is an easy, accurate way to transfer such marks as pocket placements and dart points. If you plan to sew the garment piece right away, and if the fabric is tightly woven enough to prevent the pins from falling out, consider using pins alone. If you think the pins might fall out, combine them with chalk or removable ink, as shown on p. 21.

Chalk, Ink, and Other Choices

There's a wide range of pencils, pens, and other tools available for marking fabric; though none of them is the perfect marker, all are useful. Pastel-colored chalks come in cakes called tailor's chalk, in pencil form, and as chalk liners. Whatever its form, chalk shows well on smooth-textured fabrics in colors that contrast with the chalk, and is easily removed from most fabrics. Tailor's chalk and pencils are soft, making it hard to get a fine line, and need to be sharpened frequently. Chalk liners are applicators filled with loose chalk, which is applied in a crisp, thin line by a tiny serrated wheel in the applicator.

A recently revived marking tool, traditional soapstone, comes in pencil form and shows up best on smooth-textured, dark or bright fabrics. The soapstone is harder and holds its point a bit longer than chalk pencils. Another traditional marker, the "hera," originated in Japan, where it was made of bamboo or carved ivory, and now comes in hard plastic. The hera's thin edge makes a sharp crease in fabric, which works well on tightly woven fabrics when scored on a hard surface but can damage delicate fabrics.

Water-soluble and air-erasable pens are quick and accurate but can stain some fabrics and spread on others, leaving unclear marks. Rubbing with a damp cloth or laundering removes water-soluble ink; air-erasable ink disappears automatically from the fabric in four or five days.

A tracing wheel used with tracing paper is a good standby for transferring lines to medium- to heavyweight fabrics. Since today's tracing papers are wax-free, they're less likely than older, waxed papers to leave permanent marks on fabric. A serrated tracing wheel may cut your paper pattern and can even damage lightweight fabrics. In addition to the tools described above, the sewing and notions catalogs listed in Resources on p. 87 frequently feature new, inventive markers that are worth trying.

Match the Method to the Fabric

So which marking method is the best? Choose the one that works on the fabric you're using. Here are a few guidelines:

- Thread-marking, though not the easiest method, works on all fabrics. This may be the only way to mark delicate fabrics (which can be damaged by other materials) and thick or textured fabrics that will hide other kinds of marks.

- A scissors' snip can be used in the seam allowances of fabrics that don't ravel easily.

- Marking with pins works well on most fabrics that aren't sheer or loosely woven.

- Almost any method can be used on medium- to heavyweight, firmly woven fabrics, provided you mark on the wrong side.

- Natural fibers accept chalk and ink more readily than synthetics, but they also stain more easily.

- Consider keeping a variety of markers on hand for the numerous marking tasks before and during garment construction.

Mark with Pins and/or Marker

Insert pin straight down through pattern and both fabric layers. Peel back top fabric layer and, from WS, insert another pin all the way into each layer next to first pin, or mark fabric's WS with marker. Pull pattern piece away to remove first pin.

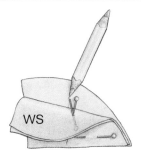

- Always mark on the fabric's wrong side, and always test the markers first on your fabric (including steam-pressing it). All of them, on occasion, can render nasty surprises with permanent stains.

- Finally, try combining methods to make marking as quick and easy as possible; for instance, use a scissors' snip in the seam allowance to mark a dart's fold- and stitching lines, and a pin or chalk mark for the dart point.

- Regardless of the tools or methods you use, the first rule of marking is, be accurate. The second rule is, be inventive and confident that if a method works for you, it works. ■

Quick Tip

Here are two quick, nontraditional ways to transfer seam allowance marks and lines with thread when other marks won't show up.

- On raw edges that will be machine finished or "serged" (which hides most other marks), mark notches, dart lines, and seamline circles with the variation of a tailor's tack shown in the drawings on the facing page.

- To hold the threads in place before they're stitched, rub the tails between your fingers with a speck of glue stick. The threads are easy to see on the finished edge, and the serging or machine stitching holds them in place.

Shrink before You Sew

a rule of thumb for handling fabrics is to prewash or dry-clean them so they do all the shrinking they are going to do before they are cut and sewn. Natural-fiber fabrics and blends shrink when washed (whether the water is cool or hot) and when steam-pressed after dry-cleaning. And drying the fabrics in a warm or hot dryer usually causes them to shrink further. Even steam-pressing during garment construction applies enough heat and moisture to a fabric to cause some shrinkage. So unless a fabric is 100 percent synthetic—or you plan to make and wear a garment without ever pressing or washing it!—always wash or dry-clean the fabric, lining and interfacing before you get out your scissors.

Quick Tip

A Note About Ironing: Once you've taken care to prewash a fabric, it will need ironing before it's cut. Iron in the direction of the straight grain (parallel with the selvage edge) to avoid stretching the fabric even slightly out of shape.

Fabric Shrinking Methods

Here's a simple guideline for deciding how to preshrink a fabric: Use the same temperatures you'll use to wash, dry, and iron the completed garment. In other words, if the garment will be washed in hot water and dried on high heat, put the fabric through a hot wash cycle (either with plain water or a little detergent) and dry it on high heat. If the garment will be hand-washed in warm water and line-dried, soak the fabric in warm water for 10 to 15 minutes so that the fibers become saturated, squeeze out (don't wring) the excess water, and hang it to dry.

To keep the wet fabric from stretching from its own weight when hung, lay it through a row of hangers, as shown in the drawing on the facing page. Even if you plan to line-dry the completed garment, if the fabric can tolerate a low-heat dry cycle, put it in a dryer to shrink it a little more. To preshrink wools and other dry-clean-only garments, take the fabric to the cleaner and have it steam-pressed. (It's possible to do this at home, but it's difficult to get reliable, uniform results.)

Preshrinking Fusible Interfacing

To prevent "interfacing failure" with bubbles in the fabric (caused by the interfacing shrinking) or bubbles in the interfacing (caused by the fabric shrinking), preshrink the interfacing you'll use. Fold it with the adhesive sides together, then soak the folded interfacing in very hot water for 20 minutes or until the water begins to cool. (Don't agitate the interfacing in the water—it will wash off the adhesive.) Gently squeeze out—don't wring—the excess water, blot with a towel, unfold the interfacing, and lay it on another towel to dry flat or through hangers to line-dry. Of course, you can't press fusible interfacing, so just before fusing the cut-out piece in place onto the appropriate prepared fashion fabric piece, give the interfacing a burst of steam from an iron an inch or so above it.

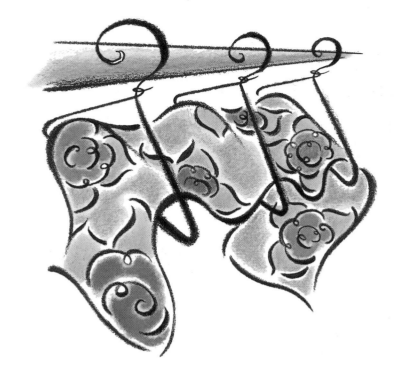

Staying Power

Once they have been preshrunk, interfacing and fabric may continue to shrink if hotter temperatures are used than the original pretreatment. Throughout the life of the garment, continue to wash, dry, and press it with the same temperatures you used in the beginning, and you won't be disappointed by any further fabric or interfacing shrinkage ▪

Quick Tip

Quick Drying Tips: While flat-drying or line-drying are always the gentlest ways to treat even the toughest fabric in a completed garment, many fabrics easily tolerate machine-drying. However, even a warm cycle can distress a fabric from abrasion as it bangs and bounces around in the dryer. To keep the finished garment looking fresh, turn it inside out before drying in the machine. Be careful to dry, not fry, that lovely fabric in the completed garment. If you leave it in the dryer until it is hot to the touch, you've removed all of the moisture from it and shortened its life.

Pattern Layouts

a well-sewn garment starts at the cutting table. Laying out your pattern on the fabric to prepare for cutting is an important step that must be done carefully and accurately for great-looking results. Here are some tips on layout and some ideas on pinning or using weights to anchor your pattern pieces in place.

Pattern Preliminaries

Be sure you have all the necessary pattern pieces. Most instruction sheets list pieces by letter or number next to the layout diagrams.

Make any changes or fitting alterations to the pattern. Press the pattern pieces with a dry iron set to a low temperature so that they're easier to work with.

Spread Out Fabric Carefully

In preparation for cutting, fabric is usually folded—be sure to spread out the fabric carefully. The instruction sheet gives alternatives for folding that are determined by the fabric's width, the garment's size, and the size of the pattern pieces. A crosswise layout is often needed for wide pieces, and sometimes a layout shows a double fold, in which both selvages are brought to the center (see

Anchor Pattern to Fabric with Pins or Weights

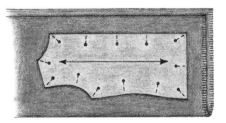

Choose pins suitable to fabric; place them perpendicular to cutting lines and pointed into corners. To keep pattern and fabric flat, catch as little of each as possible.

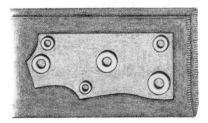

Weights are a fast, easy way to anchor a pattern. You can use weights designed for this purpose, or raid your cupboard for soup cans or something smooth and heavy enough to hold your pattern in place.

the drawings at right). In all cases, fold fabric right sides out to view designs that must be centered or matched and when cutting pile fabrics like velvet or corduroy because there's less sliding.

Choose a layout from the appropriate instruction sheet, or invent your own. When working with a plaid fabric, lay out your pattern pieces on a single thickness for easier matching, regardless of suggested layout. When laying out soft sheers and slippery fabrics, tightly cover your cutting surface with a muslin-like fabric to help prevent sliding, and use a single-thickness layout. For cutting pile fabrics, see p. 26.

Whether you fold or cut singly, always keep the entire length of fabric on top of the cutting surface while pinning and cutting to prevent distortion or stretching caused by the weight of the fabric hanging over the table's edge. For large fabric pieces, fold or roll up the end that's not being cut, and unroll as your layout progresses.

When your pattern pieces are properly aligned on the fabric, anchor them with pins, as most sewers do, or use weights, like Weight Mates (available from Clotilde or Joanne's Notions; see Resources on p. 87). See the drawings on the facing page for more on pinning and weights. Be sure that all of your pattern pieces fit on your fabric before you begin cutting. Then get out your scissors. You're ready to cut. ■

For cutting pile fabrics, see p. 26.

Choose a Cutting Layout

Pattern instructions provide layout diagrams for various fabric widths. Find the best layout in the instructions for your pattern, size, and fabric width. Here are two uncommon situations.

Without-Nap Layout, Crosswise Fold

In a without-nap layout, the pattern pieces can be placed in opposing directions.

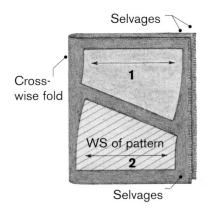

Selvages

Crosswise fold

1

WS of pattern

2

Selvages

Lengthwise Double Fold

This layout is used when two pieces fit side by side on the fabric but both need to be placed on the fold for cutting.

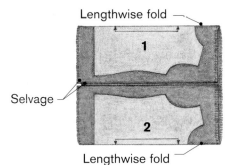

Lengthwise fold

1

Selvage

2

Lengthwise fold

With-Nap Layout Basics

the sewing term "nap" refers to the raised fibers on the surface of many fabrics that have undergone a napping process to finish one or both sides. Napped fabrics can be woven or knit and made from many different fibers. Wool and cotton flannel, melton cloth, camel's hair, mohair, cotton sweatshirt fleece, brushed denim, and even Ultrasuede®, a nonwoven synthetic fabric, all have nap.

Pile fabrics like chenille, corduroy, terry cloth, velour, and velvet are knitted or woven with an extra set of yarns to make a looped pile on one or both sides that may or may not be cut. These fabrics reflect light differently and often look richer and deeper in color when seen from one direction versus another. Both napped and pile fabrics—as well as any one-way print or a woven fabric that looks different from various directions—must be cut out with all of the pattern pieces lying in the same direction, top to bottom.

This is called a "with-nap" layout. Use a with-nap layout for pile fabrics, like velvet and corduroy, and for satin and fabrics with a definite one-way design. A "without-nap" layout is used when pattern pieces can be laid in both directions. If you cut without regard to nap, as the generic issue is referred to, some sections of your garment will appear a different shade of color or will have the printed design upside down.

Carefully consider nap when you purchase fabric. Cutting a with-nap layout sometimes requires more fabric, and the required yardage will be indicated on the pattern envelope.

Which Direction Is Correct?

Begin the process of choosing the direction in which the nap or pile will run on the finished garment with a "stroke test": Rub your hand over the fabric following the straight of grain, or selvage edge. If the surface feels smooth,

Cut pile fabrics such as corduroy using a with-nap layout, laying all the pattern pieces in the same direction, since corduroy reflects light differently and looks richer in color with the pile running up the fabric (left) rather than down (right).

Nap, Pile, and Layout

Lay pattern pieces with hems in same direction for with-nap fabric. If layout calls for folding fabric crosswise, fold fabric RSs together, cut in half, and rotate top layer 180 degrees to keep nap direction consistent.

With-Nap Layout

For Fabric Folded Crosswise

Selvages

Pants back

60-in.-wide fabric

Pants front

Fold

Waistband
(Cut on single layer.)

you're brushing with the nap or pile; if it feels rough, you're brushing against it. Many sewers cut napped fabrics with the nap running from the top of the garment down (that is, with the nap), so the nap stays flat and the fabric wears better. As well, they often cut pile fabrics with the pile running from the hem up (against the pile), so the fabric looks darker and richer. You can cut out the garment with the nap or pile running in either direction, provided you're consistent.

To help you decide how you want to cut your fabric, drape it around your neck with the ends hanging down (the nap, pile, or pattern will run down one side and up the other) and study the effect in a mirror. Which side do you like best? Mark the top or bottom of the fabric as your choice and place the pattern pieces accordingly.

As a rule, use a "with-nap" layout for all fabrics. If short of fabric for a with-nap layout, carefully check the fabric's appearance using the mirror test before turning any pattern pieces and cutting a without-nap layout.

Many prints, stripes, and some woven designs like balanced twills and certain herringbones that don't appear at first glance to require a nap layout often do have a subtle difference in appearance.

If the layout requires folding the fabric crosswise instead of lengthwise in order to produce a with-nap layout, cut the fabric in half crosswise and turn one layer to keep the nap running in the same direction on both pieces (see the drawing above right). But before cutting the fabric in half crosswise, place all the pattern pieces on the fabric to ensure that there's enough fabric to cut out the entire garment. If you're short of fabric for a with-nap layout, you can probably save fabric by cutting each piece separately, with the fabric spread in a single layer. Be sure to turn the pattern pieces over so you have both right and left pieces for your garment. Taking extra precautions with these special fabrics will ensure great results. ■

Cutting Out

a well-sewn garment cannot make up for carelessness at the cutting table. Accurate cutting doesn't have to be difficult if you keep in mind a few simple things.

Tools and Tables

Don't compromise when it comes to scissors. A good-quality pair of sharp, bent-handled shears that allows the fabric to lie flat on the table is necessary for accurate cutting. There

are many types and styles of scissors to choose from, and you may want to have more than one pair. The Softouch spring-action scissors by Fiskars™ are lightweight and have a comfortable handle, which is suitable for left- or right-handed sewers. They work best on light- to medium-weight fabrics.

Some sewers prefer to use a rotary cutter rather than scissors. It takes a little practice to get the hang of using a rotary cutter, but once you do, it's fast and accurate. Rotary cutters are available with blades in various sizes beginning with $1\frac{1}{8}$ in. (28 mm) and should be replaced or sharpened with a rotary-blade sharpener when they get dull (see Resources on p. 87). Use a hard plastic ruler to hold down the pattern and fabric and to guide the cutting blade when cutting long, straight edges. And switch to sharp scissors when cutting tight corners or small curves. Always use a mat that's especially designed for rotary cutting on a table surface (see the photo on the facing page).

Table height is also an important consideration. A table that's about 34 in. high, or 4 in. higher than a standard dining table, makes cutting easier and is better for your back. Of course, this depends on your height. Portable cutting tables are available at many fabric stores or by mail order. If

Use bent-handled shears, and cut with pattern and fabric to the left of the scissors (vice versa for lefties). Cut with long, steady strokes along the cutting line using the entire blade of the scissors. And keep the fabric flat on the table.

possible, position your table so you can approach it from both sides for easier cutting.

Cutting Reminders

- Keep the entire length of fabric folded on the table (not draped over the edge) while you cut, so the grain of the fabric will not be distorted.

- Most of the time, it's more efficient to fold the fabric and cut two layers at once. Sometimes, though, it's easier and more accurate to cut a single layer at a time— for example, when the fabric is heavy or especially delicate and hard to control or when cutting plaids and other designs that need matching.

- When cutting single layers, always be sure to turn the pattern tissue over to cut the second piece; otherwise, you'll end up with two right or two left sections. And to save time, get in the habit of cutting everything at once—interfacings, linings, and so on.

Direction Makes a Difference

- If you're right-handed, cut with the pattern and fabric to the left of your scissors. (Reverse this if you're left-handed.) This way you can clearly see the cutting lines while supporting the pattern and fabric with your left hand. If you can't reach around each pattern piece to cut in this way, roughly cut around the sections to separate them. Turn the roughly cut pieces to find the best cutting position.

- On straight cutting lines and large curves, cut with long, steady strokes using the entire blade of the scissors. On small curves, use shorter strokes. Cut exactly along the cutting lines, and don't lift the fabric as you cut.

A rotary cutter provides a fast, accurate way to cut out patterns. Use a ruler as a guide on straight edges, and always use a protective cutting mat.

- Whenever possible, cut from the widest part of the pattern to the narrowest. For example, cut the side seams of an A-line skirt from hem to waist; cut the seams of a fitted sleeve from underarm to hem.

- Pay attention to the pattern notches while cutting. They're important for matching one cut garment section to another. If you're a beginning sewer, cut all notches outward, as indicated on the pattern, cutting double and triple notches in one unit. More experienced sewers often cut straight through notches, then mark them on the fabric with a snip or a chalk mark. Don't cut notches toward the seam because this cuts away too much of the seam allowance and weakens it.

- Pay careful attention to your cutting; your reward will be easier, more accurate sewing. It's a simple, worthwhile equation. ■

Preventive Sewing-Machine Maintenance

most sewing-machine problems can be traced to poor general maintenance or neglect. But with some simple tools and just a few minutes daily, weekly, or monthly—depending on how much you're sewing—you can help keep your machine running smoothly. Here are some guidelines for care that should keep you and your machine happy and out of the repair shop.

Keep It Covered

Dust, lint, grit, and animal hair can find their way into your machine and cause all sorts of problems, especially for the printed circuit board of a computerized machine. So try not to place it near an open window, and always cover it when not in use. You can purchase a ready-made plastic cover from a notions or machine dealer, make one yourself, or even use an old pillowcase.

Caring for your sewing machine requires only a few simple tools available from your machine dealer or fabric store: A small lint brush, a can of ozone-friendly compressed air, a clean piece of muslin, sewing-machine oil, and a dust cover.

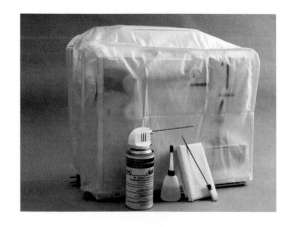

Change Your Needles Often

Professional sewers recommend replacing the needle after every four hours of sewing time. When you sew, the needle passes through the fabric thousands of times per minute, and each time it does two things: It makes a hole in the fabric for the thread to glide through, and it forms a loop with the thread to make the actual stitch. The bobbin hook picks up this loop by moving just 0.05 mm or less behind the needle—about the thickness of a piece of paper—so if the needle becomes bent or dull, you may get skipped stitches, broken or looped threads, runs and pulls in the fabric, or even damage to your machine.

When the needle is compatible with your fabric and thread, your machine sews more smoothly. An inappropriate needle will force the thread through the fabric instead of letting it glide cleanly through the needle hole and may cause broken or sheared threads. A common mistake is to use a needle that's too small for the thread. For example, a size 70/10 needle is the right choice for many thin fabrics; use a size 60 or 65 with fine, lightweight thread, like lingerie thread.

A sharp needle, like a Microtex or jeans needle, is the better choice when sewing natural-fiber woven fabrics than the universal needle, which has a slight ballpoint and was developed to glide between synthetic polyester fibers without breaking them.

Regular ballpoint needles, however, are still the best for sewing knits, fleece fabrics, and elastic. And now there are needles specially designed for sewing with rayon or metallic threads; they have Teflon®-coated eyes to reduce friction and thread breakage.

Wind Bobbins Correctly

Be sure there are no thread tails hanging from the bobbin when it's inserted into the bobbin case. They can jam the machine and cause the upper thread to break. And note that there's no such thing as a generic bobbin. Always use a bobbin designed for your machine in order to avoid skipped stitches, loose threads, and noise, as well as permanent damage to the bobbin case.

Regular Cleaning Is Essential

Get in the habit of cleaning your machine after each project. Follow the instructions in your manual, or ask your machine mechanic to show you how. Basically, a routine cleaning can be accomplished quickly and easily if you follow these steps:

STEP 1. Start at the top and clean the tension disks with a folded piece of fine muslin (see the left photo, above). Be sure the presser foot is up, so the tension springs are loose and the muslin can move easily between the disks, dislodging any lint or fuzz.

STEP 2. Use a can of compressed air, blowing from back to front, to remove loose particles from around the tension disks and to clean other areas inside the machine. Don't blow into your machine yourself because breath contains moisture and will eventually cause corrosion.

STEP 3. Get into the habit of removing the machine's needle and throwing it away after completing a project. Then take out the throat plate, bobbin, bobbin case, and hook race if this applies to your machine (new computerized machines do not have removable hooks).

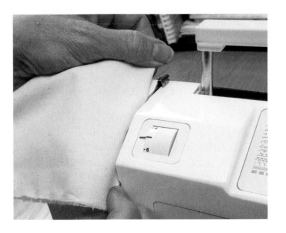

Fold a piece of muslin in half, and use the folded edge to clean between tension disks.

Don't forget to clean inside the bobbin case. Using compressed air, which has a straw (shown in red, above) to direct air to a desired spot, blow out lint and loose threads.

STEP 4. Clean under the feed dogs and around the bobbin area with a small brush, and use the compressed air to blow out any lint from inside of the bobbin case (see the right photo above).

STEP 5. If the hook mechanism is removable, wipe it clean with a dot of oil on a piece of muslin (see the photo at right), and give it an additional small drop of oil before returning it to the machine. Use a light oil recommended for sewing machines; do not use three-in-one oil. Check with your manual regarding any other areas on your machine that may require oiling, and use only a small drop for each spot. It is always better to oil too little more often than too much at one time, and avoid oiling any plastic parts.

You can easily do this routine by yourself, but in addition, take your machine for a check-up by your dealer or an authorized mechanic every two years. Your machine will give you years of service if you take the time to care for it properly. ■

Use a soft piece of muslin with a dot of sewing machine oil to clean the race hook. If the hook is removable, place a drop of oil on it before returning it to the machine.

Sewing notions. Who knew it could be so complicated. Take pins, for example, flower-head, dressmaker's, silk, ballpoint, universal. Which should you buy? Or those oddly shaped feet that guide the fabric through the machine—if only you knew what to do with them. Or the dizzying variety of threads in the shops—does it really matter if you use cotton or silk or polyester? The reason for all the variety is that each size, shape, or composition makes the sewing of a particular fabric go smoothly…or not. Once you learn the basics, it won't seem complicated at all and you'll appreciate the care with which these items have been developed to aid in specific sewing tasks. ■

part 2

Needle and Thread

Straight Pins

Pins are pins, right? Well, not exactly—especially if you've looked at the array of pins offered in mail-order sewing catalogs. There are silk pins, dressmaker's pins, quilter's pins, all-purpose pins, and appliqué and knitter's pins. The names given to pins generally describe their length and diameter, as well as their intended use: Pins with a small diameter (0.5 mm to 0.55 mm) are intended for use with lightweight, delicate fabrics, and pins with a larger diameter (0.6 mm) are intended for medium- to heavyweight fabrics.

Quality pins are made from stainless steel or nickel-plated steel. Unlike stainless steel, nickel-plated steel (generally labeled "steel" on the packaging) may rust over time,

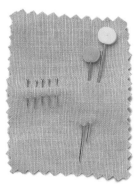

especially when left in fabric. Plated steel is used in some plastic-head pins and must be used for glass-head pins because glass won't bond to stainless steel.

Pin Points

Let logic prevail when choosing a straight pin: Select a pin to suit the fabric—the finer the fabric, the finer the pin should be or it will leave large, unsightly holes. You want pins that stay put and are comfortable and convenient to use. Most sewers are practical people; finger size and agility override strict pin rules. The bottom line? Use any pin for any purpose that works!

- Silk pins (top photo on the facing page), also called dressmaker's or superfine silk pins, are 0.5 mm in diameter and 1¼ in. to 1⅜ in. long. Silk pins are good for most light- to medium-weight fabrics and serve well in tight corners where a longer pin might get in the way—and glass-head silk pins don't hide in the carpet as readily as their flat-headed cousins!

- Quilting, or all-purpose, pins (bottom right on the facing page) are 0.6 mm in

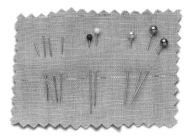

Storing and Caring for Pins

Most sewers eventually acquire a variety of pins to suit different sewing situations, and keep them sorted by type and stored in some sort of holder or stuffed pincushions. Many sewers prefer magnetic pin holders because they'll grab a pin tossed at them from a few inches away and quickly retrieve spilled pins. Though most electronic sewing machines don't seem to be affected by the magnets, it's advisable not to place a magnetic holder directly on your machine.

Since pins are cheap, buy those of good quality, and if one gets bent, nicked, or rusted, just pitch it. Be sure to keep pins out of your mouth, and never, but never, sew over a pin. If you *must* sew over a pin, move the flywheel by hand until you're safely past it. ▪

diameter and 1½ in. to 1¾ in. long. The large heads on quilting and all-purpose pins make them easy to grasp, and their length helps them stay in position in thick fabrics and quilts.

- Flower-head pins (below) are 1⅞ in. long and have a diameter of 0.55 mm, which makes them more flexible than all-purpose or regular quilting pins or the stout and sturdy 2-in.-long, 1-mm-thick quilting pins. Flower-head pins are useful for laces and loosely woven fabric because they're easy to grasp and won't get lost in the fabric.

- Tiny appliqué pins (the small pins on the facing page), won't snag your thread when hand-sewing appliqué pieces.

- Knitter's pins (shown next to the appliqué pins on the facing page) are long, large, and dull-pointed, so they'll stay in position in bulky knits but they won't pierce a knit's yarns.

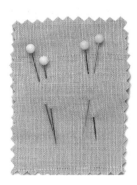

The Secrets of Machine Needles

Sewing-machine needles may be your most important sewing notions—the size, type, and condition of these tiny giants determine how well your machine forms a stitch. To do this properly, the needle has to penetrate the fabric and deliver its thread to the bobbin at exactly the right spot so that the two threads can form a loop and pull it tight. Your needle must accomplish this precision feat on all kinds of fibers—from tissue-thin silk to multiple layers of denim using plain and fancy stitches, and regular and novelty threads.

To meet these specialized demands, needle manufacturers have engineered subtle modifications into the needle's basic anatomy. Take a side-by-side look at several different needles and you'll appreciate these details, such as the point shaping and eye. All needle points are variously shaped to push the different fibers aside rather than cut through them. The long notches or "scarf depths" on needles are designed to accommodate different fabrics to ensure forming a proper loop. Eyes and front grooves are variously sized and shaped to handle a range of thread types and diverse sewing situations.

Needle Names

When selecting a needle for a project, first consider the type of needle you'll need, then its size. In general, a needle's name describes the fabric or special sewing it's designed for or the type of special thread used with it. Here are a few of the basic needles:

- Denim and leather needles are intended for those fabrics.

- Universals work on most woven and knit fabrics and cover most sewing situations.

- Ballpoints are designed for heavy knits, double knits, and synthetic-blend interlocks (but not for synthetic wovens).

- Stretch needles are made for highly elastic knits like Lycra™, and synthetic nonwovens like Ultrasuede.

- Mictrotex/sharps stitch well on microfiber fabrics and other fine-fiber, tightly woven fabrics like sand-washed rayon.

- Topstitching (sometimes labeled system) needles have large eyes for heavy, decorative threads.

- Machine-embroidery needles have an elongated eye suited to decorative rayon and fine-cotton embroidery threads.

- The groove and eye on Metallica and Metalfil needles are designed for metallic threads.

- Quilting needles sew through multiple layers of fabric, seams, and batting.

- A variety of double and triple needles are used for decorative stitching.

- Wing needles are used for heirloom sewing.

- Most sergers take standard universal needles, but some require special serger needles as recommended by the manufacturer.

Needle Numbers

Needle sizes range from 60/8 to 120/19, but not all needle types come in all sizes. The dual numbers indicate first the European size, then its U.S. equivalent. For instance, the European number 100 in a size 100/16 indicates the size of wire used to make the needle. So all size 100/16 needles begin life as a 1-mm wire, regardless of the type of needle they become. In general, 60/8 needles are used on very lightweight, 70/12 on lightweight, 80/12 on medium-weight, 90/14 on heavyweight, and 100/16 on very heavyweight fabrics.

Fresh Needle Logic

A bent, dull, or nicked needle is responsible for most skipped or tangled stitches and broken or frayed threads. These needle blemishes are hard to spot with the naked eye, so if your stitch goes bad, first see if the machine is clean and properly threaded. If the problem persists, changing the needle will usually cure it.

Many sewers routinely install a fresh needle for a new project, but why retire a needle if it looks perfectly good? Consider that 60 percent of needles are discarded during manufacture because of flaws measured in fractions of a millimeter—such are the minuscule tolerances for the best performance from a needle. From a microscopic point of view, imagine the beating that a needle takes as it bangs past fibers hundreds of times a minute, and how a damaged needle reduces stitch quality. Then remember that a fresh needle of the right size and type for the task at hand ensures consistently beautiful stitches. ■

Anatomy of a Needle

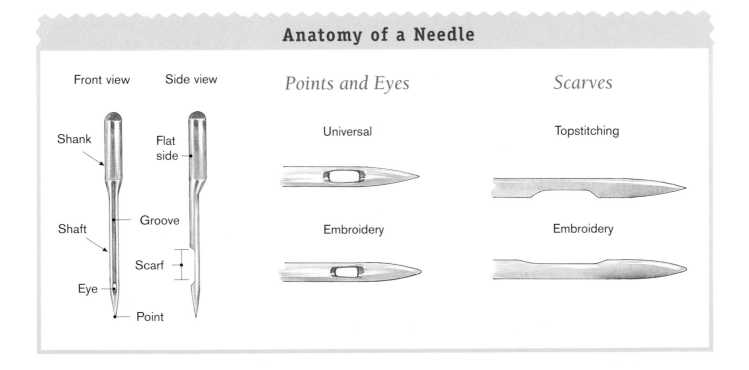

Front view   Side view

Shank
Flat side
Shaft
Groove
Scarf
Eye
Point

Points and Eyes

Universal

Embroidery

Scarves

Topstitching

Embroidery

Presser Feet

Whether you inherited your grandmother's treasured sewing machine or recently bought a new one, chances are it came with a puzzling array of presser feet. The most recognizable feet are those for straight and zigzag stitching, making button-holes, and applying zippers. Additional feet commonly sold with sewing machines include those for blind hems, rolled hems, overlocking, and darning. Each foot is designed to make a specific sewing task easier and more successful by helping feed the fabric past the needle (while sometimes shaping it).

To better understand why so many different feet are necessary, let's look at what they do. First, a presser foot is designed to press the fabric against the feed dogs as they pull the fabric under the needle—two exceptions are the darning and free-motion-embroidery feet, used with the feed dogs down, allowing the fabric to be guided by hand. Second, a presser foot must let the completed stitches pass smoothly from under it to the back of the sewing machine.

Anatomy of a Presser Foot

Presser feet intended for sewing with the feed dogs up all have much the same basic anatomy: The shank, which is either built into the machine or is part of the foot itself, attaches the foot to the machine. The ball joint, if there is one, provides a pivot point that allows the foot to move over uneven

Parts of a Presser Foot

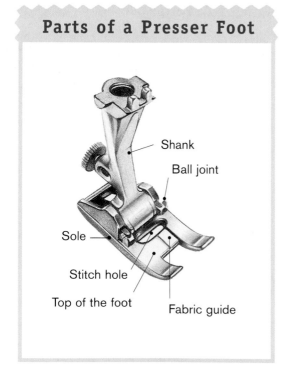

Shank

Ball joint

Sole

Stitch hole

Top of the foot

Fabric guide

fabric thicknesses. The top of the foot is contoured to guide or shape the fabric under the needle properly for the assigned sewing task. The stitch hole is either wide to accommodate the needle's widest sideways movement or position, or very narrow to prevent up and down movement of delicate fabrics as the needle passes through them.

The sole is the underside of the foot and includes the thread escape, which helps guide the fabric behind the needle and allows it to move freely out the back of the foot. The thread escape's configuration varies from foot to foot, depending upon the foot's intended task.

The escape may be short and narrow like the universal foot to accommodate flat, narrow stitches, such as for straight-stitched seams. Or on presser feet intended for wide, thick, decorative or satin stitching, like the open embroidery foot, a wide thread escape extends to the back of the foot to allow the fabric and stitches to move freely under the foot. Presser feet designed for cording, rolled hems, buttonholes, or other thick, narrow stitching, have deeply grooved thread escapes so the fabric passes evenly under the needle and out the back.

Why not get acquainted with the different presser feet that came with your machine by practicing their uses as shown in the machine's instruction manual? You may find the perfect solution to a sewing challenge that your regular foot is simply not equal to. ◾

Task-Driven Design

While all presser feet contain the same basic parts, each foot's design is determined by its function and may vary from brand to brand. For example, the fabric guide on the Bernina® blind-stitch foot is a thin metal fence, while that on the Pfaff™ clip-on blind-stitch foot is an adjustable red edge guide. The shape and position of the thread escape on the sole, or underside of a foot, vary with the foot's task.

Blind-stitch feet (Bernina, left, and Pfaff, right)

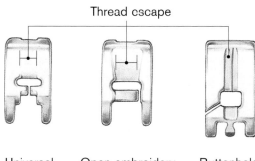

Thread escape

Universal foot   Open embroidery foot   Buttonhole foot

Construction Threads

Shopping for garment-construction thread was easy in the days when there was one kind of thread available in a limited number of colors. The only trick was to find the best color to match your fabric! Nowadays it's not quite that simple—most fabric stores carry a daunting array of threads for your sewing machine in different fiber contents and weights and in a wonderful choice of colors. Here are guidelines to help you purchase the right garment-construction thread for the job.

What Color?

The construction thread should be the same color but one shade darker than the fabric so the thread blends as invisibly as possible. If you can't find a good color match, look for a gray or other neutral color that's the same value as or slightly darker than the fabric. When the stitches are visible in a pressed seam (which is unavoidable on some fabrics), a neutral color a shade darker than the fabric will show less than a much lighter or darker thread the same color as the fabric.

Match the Thread's Strength to the Fabric

When selecting a construction thread, a consideration even more important than color is the thread's strength. As a rule, avoid a thread that's stronger than the fabric so that if a seam rips under stress when worn, it will be the thread, and not the fabric, that gives way. Reinforce seams that will receive stress during wear (for example, in the underarm or crotch) with a stronger thread or by stitching the seam twice. The following are commonly used construction threads.

Polyester—The fiber in all-polyester thread is strong, resistant to abrasion, and has good stretch and recovery properties. Polyester is a good, all-purpose thread for knits and synthetic blends. As well, it's the best choice for taffetas and bridal satins, heavy wools, gabardines, denims, and heavy cottons such as duck. Garment-construction threads for the serger are 100-percent polyester and a somewhat finer weight than sewing-machine poly. (Another garment-construction thread for the serger is woolly nylon, an all-nylon specialty thread used only in the loopers.)

Cotton—Cotton thread is soft, with little or no elasticity, and is the best choice for most natural-fiber woven fabrics. Cotton has the advantage of creasing and melding into a seam when pressed, producing a beautiful, flat seam. (To see this in action, fold a length of polyester thread in half and crease the fold, then do the same with cotton thread. You'll see a definite crease in the cotton and almost no crease in the polyester.)

Cotton threads are identified by a number, such as 50/3, which designates the strand size (the higher the number, the smaller the strand) and then the number of strands. The most commonly available cotton threads for garment construction are 50/3, good for most natural-fiber woven fabrics, and 60/2, which produces a good seam on very lightweight fabrics.

Cotton-wrapped polyester—Cotton-wrapped polyester, the most widely available all-purpose thread, has an inner polyester core with a short-staple cotton outer cover, which makes it slightly weaker than its all-polyester cousin. Cotton-wrapped polyester thread can be linty, and the difference in elasticity between the two fibers requires extra care when winding the bobbin and set-ting tensions. But this thread is a workable compromise for most woven fabrics.

Silk—Silk thread is best used for marking and basting delicate fabrics because its smooth fibers don't damage a fabric's fine yarns and weaves. However, because silk thread is even stronger than polyester, it should be used for garment construction only on equally strong or heavyweight fabrics.

Quality Counts

Consider using the best threads your budget will allow. The thread's appearance on the spool is a good indication of its quality. If it looks fuzzy, it's probably made from a short-staple fiber, which is weaker than the long-staple fibers used in better threads, creates more lint, and causes a loss of stitch quality as it feeds unevenly through the machine. Remember, there are no absolutes in selecting garment-construction thread but choosing the best thread for the project will provide a visible improvement in the finished product. ▪

Must-Have Tools

Point presser and clapper

good tools are an extension of your sewing machine and basic for any sewing room. They make most tasks easier, improve results, and certainly add to sewing enjoyment. But there are so many great gadgets available today, how do you choose tools that are really effective and useful and won't just clutter your toolbox? A good tool is one with a simple design that easily accomplishes the task it was meant to do, and it's one that you reach for over and over.

Shown here are five tools you may find you absolutely could not live without.

They're all inexpensive items that you can find in most notions departments, or see Resources on p. 87.

Bamboo Point Turner and Creaser

This little, unassuming tool costs around $2. Its pointed end is used to poke the point when turning corners right side out, and its rounded, beveled end smoothes out curved seams. The soft wood minimally stresses fabric and stitching, yet gently helps form a crisp corner or curve. You can even insert it into a point or curve as you press a seam.

1

3

Bamboo point turner and creaser (1)

Open-toe appliqué foot (2)

Loop turner (3)

Buttonhole gauge (4)

2

4

Buttonhole Gauge

This exotic device, which costs around $15, looks complex but actually simplifies positioning and measuring buttonholes, pleats, tucks, or anything else needing to be evenly spaced. It's a great time-saver, because it eliminates the need for calculating and carefully measuring intervals. It's easy to use—simply mark the position of the top and bottom buttonhole, for example, and stretch the gauge to fit.

Open-Toe Appliqué Foot

What a great idea—a presser foot that's open in the front so you can actually see what you're stitching. This is an accessory that's available for most sewing machines, but there are also generic varieties in metal or clear plastic for low-shank, high-shank, and slant-shank machines. The price can vary depending on your machine, but the generic feet range from around $5 to $15. Some open-toe appliqué feet also have a cutaway channel underneath that allows the foot to slide easily over dense satin stitches. It's great for all kinds of precision sewing like topstitching. It's especially useful when you want to make sure topstitching meets precisely at corners.

Point Presser and Clapper

Here's an invaluable piece of equipment that sells for around $20. It's a classic, hardwood pressing tool that's really two tools in one. The top, narrow-surfaced, point presser side works like a tiny ironing board for pressing hard-to-reach seams and enclosed corners, like those on collars, lapels, and cuffs.

The bottom, clapper side is used to apply pressure to set permanent creases, form crisp edges, and flatten bulky seams. To use it, first apply steam to the area with your iron, then press with the clapper, leaning on it and applying as much pressure as possible. Hold this position until both the fabric and wood (which presses the steam into the area without adding heat) have cooled.

If you don't already have these great tools, consider adding them to your sewing box. They'll soon become your favorites, too. ■

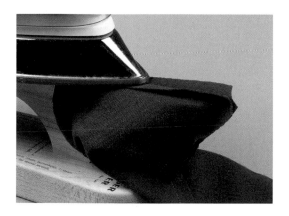

A point presser is invaluable for pressing hard-to-reach seams. Slip the seam, wrong side up, over the point and press open.

To use a loop turner, insert the long wire through a narrow fabric tube; hook the end, close the latch, and pull the hooked-end to the right side.

Yes, the sewing machine does a lot of the work for you, but you need to know how to set it for the task at hand and what to do to make a seam lie smoothly in the garment. Here you'll learn about different stitch types and when to use them, how to sew a seam the right way, how to trim and press seams for professional results, and even how to rip out mistakes without damaging your work. In addition, you'll learn how to sew in zippers, make darts, gathers, and pleats—you'll even learn to make decorative piping. These are all basic sewing skills that will serve you well no matter what type of sewing project you take on.

part 3

Perfect Seams

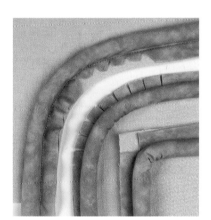

Staystitching

Staystitching is a term often seen in pattern instructions but rarely defined. You may be inclined to ignore this step because you don't know why it's necessary or how to do it effectively—or maybe you just don't want to take the time. But it's such an important step because it prevents curved or angled edges from stretching out of shape as you construct the garment, resulting in smooth, even curves and accurate, balanced seams.

What Is Staystitching?

Staystitching is a row of permanent, straight stitches sewn on cut-out garment pieces before they're seamed together. The stitching is usually done ⅛ in. inside the seam allowance (½ in. from the cut edge on ⅝-in. seam allowances). The best time to staystitch is immediately after you've transferred the pattern markings to the cut piece and removed the pattern tissue.

Where to Staystitch?

As a general rule, curved and slightly bias edges require staystitching because these areas can easily be stretched both while you're working on the garment and when you wear it. In a blouse, for example, the neckline, shoulder, armhole, and tapered sleeve seams should be staystitched. (A sleeve cap, although curved, doesn't need staystitching because it will be eased or possibly gathered to fit into the armhole, and you want a certain amount of give here.) Unlike bias-cut edges, those cut on the straight or crossgrain (like many side seams and hems) don't need to be staystitched because they don't stretch easily.

If you're making a straight skirt, however, the slightly curved waistline seam and side seams above the hipline should be staystitched to prevent stretching during fitting and sewing. These same areas (waistline and hipline) should be staystitched in pants along with the curved crotch seam and the slightly bias upper section of the inseam.

If you're making a skirt that's designed to be cut on the bias, it's not necessary to

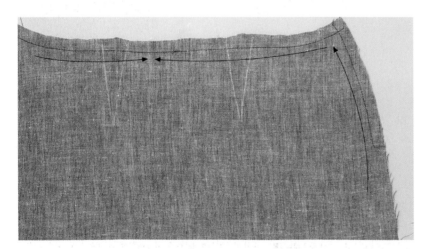

To prevent stretching while fitting and sewing straight skirts and pants, staystitch the slightly curved waistline and hip sections of the side seams. (Avoid distortion by staystitching with the fabric's grain, as noted by the arrows.)

staystitch the side seams. In this case, you want the slight stretch that results from the bias cut. If you "stayed" this area, the soft drape would be lost.

For Best Results

- Use the same thread and stitch length that you'll use for sewing the garment seams (generally 10–12 sts/in.).

- Since you'll staystitch on a single thickness, sew a test row on a scrap of your fabric to check for correct tension.

- To be sure that your staystitching is accurate and straight, sew with the cut edge of the garment piece along the ½-in. guide mark on the throat plate.

- Be careful not to stretch the edges as you staystitch.

- And, finally, there's no need to backstitch when staystitching.

Directional Stitching

The direction in which you staystitch is important. Always try to sew in the direction of the fabric's grain because sewing against the grain may cause distortion. To determine grain direction, run your finger along the cut edge of the garment piece. If the yarns lie smoothly, the direction is with the grain; if the yarns "stand up," it's against the grain.

A garment section may have several edges that need staystitching. To staystitch with the grain on all these edges, you can't start at one point and continuously stitch to the end point. Instead, you need to staystitch each edge separately. For example, on a front bodice, sew each shoulder from neckline to armhole, as shown by the arrows in the photo at right. Then sew half of the neckline from the shoulder to center front, flip the bodice, and sew the other half from shoulder to center front. Sew each armhole from shoulder to side seam.

Staystitch, on a single thickness, any curved or slightly bias-cut edge that's likely to stretch. Stitch ⅛ in. inside the seam allowance, using the throat-plate guide for straight, even lines.

Staystitching Bonus

Many curved areas require clipping after seaming so that they'll lie flat when pressed. Staystitching gives you a point to clip to and stays and strengthens the seamline to be clipped. And, if you ever need to alter your garment, the staystitching acts as a stabilizer when the seams are taken apart.

Why not start every project with staystitching? It takes little time and effort, and the results are worth it! ■

Staystitch in the direction of the fabric grain to prevent the fabric from stretching. On a front bodice, for example, as indicated by the arrows, stitch the shoulder from neckline to armhole; the neckline from shoulder to center front; and the armhole from shoulder to side seam.

Sew a Perfect Seam from Beginning to End

Since the seam is the basic element used to join the various pieces of a garment, most sewing instructions include the seemingly simple direction, "Pin the two edges of fabric right sides together and sew the seam." But starting a seam neatly and accurately is often a challenge for experienced and new sewers alike: The needle may push the fabric down into the throat plate hole, the beginning of a seam may bunch up, the thread may get tangled, or any backstitching used may look wrinkled. At the other end of the seam, the problems are fewer but not entirely absent. Below are some suggestions for sewing a seam that's perfect from beginning to end.

Starting the Seam

One approach to neatly starting a seam involves, first, placing the fabric under the presser foot and turning the handwheel twice to anchor the thread in the fabric. Next, use one hand to guide the fabric in front of the presser foot and the other hand to hold the threads behind the presser foot (see the photo below). Then backstitch once or twice (no more, or you'll create unnecessary bulk in the seam) to lock the beginning of the seam, and stitch forward, pulling the threads behind the presser foot to get the seam smoothly under way. If the top of a seam will be trimmed later to reduce bulk, be careful to place the backstitching about ½ in. from the top raw edge so it won't be lost in trimming.

Another good way to start a seam, which works with all weights and types of fabric, begins with a 3-in. square of lightweight muslin. Fold the square in half and place the strip lengthwise under the presser foot at midstrip, aligning its long raw edges with the correct seam guideline on the throat plate (see the top photo on the facing page). Start stitching, and as you come to the strip's bottom end, stop and line up the beginning of the garment seam with the strip. Sew onto the fabric, backstitch once or twice, then

To get a seam under way without problem, try gently pulling the bobbin and needle threads as you sew, after first anchoring the thread by turning the handwheel for a few stitches and then taking a backstitch or two.

complete the seam. This method gives you something to hold as you begin the seam and enables you to sew it evenly. Later, just clip away the muslin.

A third way to start a seam is to pin a 3-in. square of paper or tear-away stabilizer at the beginning of the seam, keeping the pins away from the seamline. Begin sewing on the paper and stitch right onto the fabric, which will feed evenly into the machine (see the bottom photo). After finishing the seam, carefully tear away the paper.

Ending a Great Seam

Paper can be used to stabilize the end of a seam as well as its start. About 2 in. from the end of the seam, with the needle down, lift the presser foot and slip the paper under the fabric. Lower the foot, continue sewing, backstitch near the end of the seam, and then tear away the paper.

Another way to end a seam, particularly in lightweight fabric, is by reducing stitch length. For the last 1 in. to 1½ in. of the seam, use 16–18 sts/in. Backstitching isn't needed, and the resulting end is smooth.

Of course, sewing a perfect seam involves more than just a good beginning and ending. To get a great stitch in-between, select a needle type and size that suits the weight and structure of your fabric, as well as a good-quality thread. Be sure to set the thread tension and stitch length so that they'll combine to produce a smooth seam. And don't forget to make a stitch sample on your garment fabric, which is worth keeping for future reference. Cut two pieces of fabric (so that you're sewing on the actual thickness of the seam), sew some test rows, and make note of the machine settings, thread, and needle that gave you the best results. ■

A folded strip of muslin makes a great "handle" to start a seam. At the bottom of the strip, align the garment seam, sew onto the fabric, backstitch twice, then complete the seam.

A pinned square of paper likewise eliminates problems at the beginning of a seam. When the seam is completed, gently tear away the paper stabilizer.

Easing in a Seam

S ewers use the term ease in two very different ways. One use describes the amount of extra room a garment provides (for comfort or style) beyond the fit of a skintight basic pattern. The other use, and the one we'll be concerned with here, refers to ease along a seam. If one seamline was intentionally cut longer than the seamline you're going to attach it to, and they're supposed to go together without gathers, pleats, or darts, you need to ease, or compress, the longer seamline to match the shorter one. Patterns are usually marked to show you exactly where ease should be positioned along the seam.

When Do You Need Ease?

Here are a few situations in which you typically need to ease a seamline. In every case, easing creates shape without any visible fullness.

- When setting in a sleeve where the sleeve cap is longer than the armhole it has to fit into.

- When joining shoulder seams and the rear shoulder is longer than the front.

- When making collars and the upper collar is longer than the undercollar.

- When shaping a lapel, and the roll line is longer than the stay tape that will hold it in.

Three Ways to Ease

You can work ease into a seam by preparing the seam before sewing, by stretching the shorter seam as you sew the pieces together, or by letting the machine ease in the longer edge as the layers move through.

Before sewing— For the most precise placement of fullness and control, the best approach is to compress the longer seamline before sewing it to the shorter one. Set your machine for its longest stitch and sew a row (or more) of machine basting in the seam allowance next to the seamline that needs easing. Pull up on the bobbin thread to draw in the fabric the precise amount you need, and tie off the threads to hold the shape. Pin the drawn-up layer to the piece you'll attach it to, and stitch with the eased side up so that you're sure to avoid stitching into the machine basting.

If you need to ease only a small amount, you can probably get away with just pinning the uneven layers together, then distributing the excess evenly over the eased area with more pins. Place the pins perpendicular to the seamline, and catch a small bite of the fabric layers just at the seamline with each pin.

Gathering to Ease

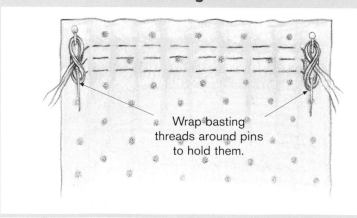

Wrap basting threads around pins to hold them.

Whether you've machine-basted or just pinned, you'll get the best results when you sew if you feed the prepared layers under the presser foot with your fingers on each side of the area being stitched. Pull slightly away from the seamline on both sides to keep the excess from bunching up in front of the foot, as shown in the top right drawing.

When minimal ease is required, steaming and pressing is another way to prepare and ease fabric pattern pieces that have been cut out before sewing them together. This approach works only on natural-fiber fabrics that can be shaped when heat and moisture are applied. Match the ends of the longer and shorter seams, steam the longer seam allowance, and then pat it gently to flatten and shape it. Press lightly to set the shaping, and let the fabric dry thoroughly before sewing.

Stretch in the ease— In some cases you can ease one layer precisely to a shorter layer simply by stretching the short one and stitching the two together while both are under tension, as shown in the bottom right drawing. This works best on stable, firmly woven fabrics and when neither edge is primarily on the bias (at the inseam of pants, for example).

To stretch in ease as you sew, begin by pinning or just holding the layers together near the marked start and end of the eased area, with the fullness positioned as you want it. Then stretch the layers until the fullness flattens out to lie flush against the short layer (the longer edge isn't stretched). Either side can be face up as you guide the layers under the foot while maintaining the same tension, but let the feed dogs actually move the fabric, or you may bend or deflect the needle as it stitches. When the stretched layer relaxes, the other layer will be evenly eased to it.

Let the machine do all the work— The least precise but still effective method for easing, especially over long seams, is

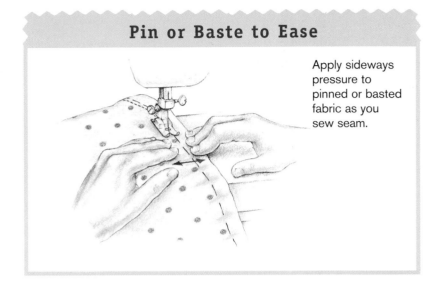

Pin or Baste to Ease

Apply sideways pressure to pinned or basted fabric as you sew seam.

simply to let the feeding mechanism of your machine ease the seam as it's sewn. While the feed dogs are pulling against the underlayer, the presser foot above is resisting the flow of the top layer, which tends to compress the underlayer and stretch the top one. (This is what even-feed and top-feed presser feet try to prevent.) To use this method, position the longer side against the feed dogs and sew the seam without applying any tension. Use few or no pins to allow the easing to proceed evenly, using your hands to keep the edges aligned. With practice, you can even increase the amount of ease by applying slight tension to just the top layer, increasing its tendency to stretch. ■

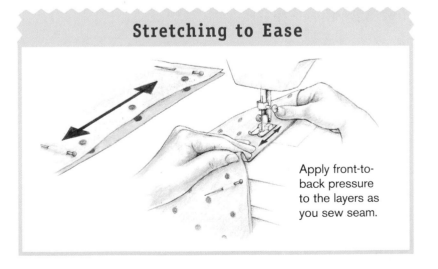

Stretching to Ease

Apply front-to-back pressure to the layers as you sew seam.

Directional Sewing

When a collar you've just sewn refuses to lie flat, like the one in the top photo on the facing page, or a neckline with beautiful topstitching ripples on one side, you might need to check the direction in which you sew these parts of the garment. Most patterns don't talk much about directional sewing, but sewing with the grain can make a big difference in your results. We're always cautioned to pay attention to the grain of the fabric when laying out a pattern, but we shouldn't stop there. It's important to continue to consider the grain while cutting, sewing, and pressing.

Cutting

Directional sewing actually starts at the cutting table. Whenever possible, cut in the direction of the fabric's grain, especially when the pattern pieces are angled or curved. The easiest way to do this is to cut from the widest part of the pattern to the narrowest— an A-line skirt from the hem to the waist, for example, or a fitted sleeve from the underarm to the wrist. Directional cutting prevents distortion of the fabric pieces and reduces fraying along the edges as well. It's not always possible to cut directionally—sometimes the position of the pattern and fabric on the table interferes—so when you need to cut against the grain, be especially careful with your scissors or rotary cutter as you work around the pattern piece.

Stitching

Beginning sewers are always amazed when they make the connection between sewing directionally and those all-important collars. Collars offer the best argument for sewing with the grain, because when sewing collars, we tend to start at one neck edge and stitch around to the other neck edge. If you sew a collar together in this way, one side will be stitched with the grain, but the other side (the one that refuses to lie flat) will be against the grain.

To sew a collar directionally, start at the center back and sew to the point, then pivot and sew to the neck edge. Remove the fabric from the machine and start again at the center back, overlapping the first few stitches a bit, sewing the collar's other side in the same way. With this method, both points will be

To determine the direction of the grain on a cut garment section, run a finger along the fabric's cut edge. The yarns will lie smoothly in the direction of the grain and "stand up" against the grain.

sewn with the grain and the collar will look exactly the same on both sides. Sew with the grain when you topstitch the collar as well.

Other parts of a garment benefit from directional stitching, too. In most cases, you can follow the same guidelines you used for cutting—stitching from the widest part to the narrowest—whether stitching seams, sewing a narrow hem along the vertical edge of a blouse front facing, or topstitching a neckline. When you can't determine what the grain direction is, run your finger gently along the cut edge. The yarns will lie smoothly in the direction of the grain, but will "stand up" against the grain.

Before you sew a garment together, however, you'll probably need to do some staystitching. Directional sewing is especially important here since it is done to hold the shape of the fabric pieces, particularly in curved areas like neckline, princess seams, waistline, and hip curves. In order to maintain the shape of each piece, it's important to staystitch in the direction of the grain.

Sometimes the grain direction changes within the garment section (like the collar) and, whether you're staystitching or sewing seams, you may need to stop, flip the fabric, and start again rather than stitch continuously around the piece. Directionally stitch the armhole seams when setting in a sleeve, especially when sewing a fabric that's particularly slippery and unstable. The sleeves will ease in more smoothly. Start at the underarm and sew to the shoulder on the front of the garment, then sew from underarm to shoulder on the back. When sewing an area like this, where you need to have a particular side of the garment facing you as you stitch, sew with the garment to the right of the needle for one-half of each armhole. This will allow you to maintain the correct stitching direction.

The only exception to directional stitching is when you're sewing a nap or pile

The importance of directional stitching is especially apparent in a collar. A collar that's stitched continuously from one neck edge to the other doesn't lie flat because only one side is sewn in the direction of the grain (top). However, the points of a directionally stitched collar, (bottom) come out exactly the same when you begin stitching at the center back and sew to the neck edge on each side.

fabric. In this case, you need to sew in the direction of the nap and can't always follow grain direction.

Pressing

You will find that directional stitching makes pressing easier because it eliminates many ripples and puckers. Try to get in the habit of pressing directionally, doing so will maintain the shape of the fabric. ■

Trimming and Grading Seams

there's more to smooth, flat seams and darts than stitching and pressing! It's often necessary to cut away some of the allowance on a seam or dart in order to reduce bulk and prevent ridges from showing on the right side of the garment. Trimming and grading—the procedures for cutting away these allowances—are explained only briefly, if at all, in commercial pattern instructions. Trimming refers to reducing any seam allowance. Grading is more specific, and is done on enclosed seams where multiple seam allowance layers create excess bulk.

Trimming

Where and when to trim a seam allowance is determined by the seam's location in the garment and the type of fabric you're using. Always check the fit of your garment before you trim.

Trim Seams and Darts to Reduce Bulk

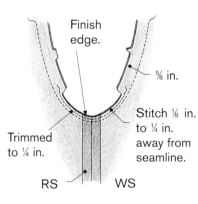

Finish edge.

⅝ in.

Stitch ⅛ in. to ¼ in. away from seamline.

Trimmed to ¼ in.

RS   WS

1. Curved underarm and crotch seams

For smoothness and to add wearing ease, stitch underarm and crotch seams ⅛ in. to ¼ in. from original seam, and trim as shown. Finish edge to prevent fraying.

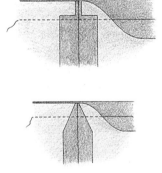

2. Intersecting seams

Trim ends of seam diagonally before intersecting seam is stitched. Or trim out corners 1⁄16 in. to ⅛ in. from stitching after seam is stitched.

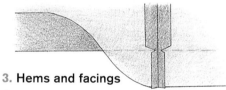

3. Hems and facings

On heavy or bulky fabrics, you may need to trim seam allowances within hem allowance or facing to reduce bulk. Taking small notches out at hemline helps hems lie flat.

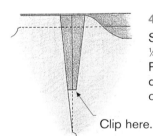

4. Darts

Slash bulky darts to ¼ in. from point. Press open top of dart and bottom to one side.

Clip here.

Seams on collars, lapels, facings, and underarms always require trimming, regardless of the fabric. As a general rule of thumb, trim seam allowances to about ¼ in. For loosely woven fabrics, trim to ⅜ in.

Curved underarm and crotch seams should be trimmed to allow for more wearing room and ease, as shown in drawing 1 on the facing page. You may also need to serge, zigzag, pink, or bind these seams' raw edges to prevent raveling.

When you're using a heavy or bulky fabric, you may need to trim seams in other areas as well, for instance, where seams intersect (see drawing 2 on the facing page) and on the seam allowances of hems and facings because the seams are layered and bulky in these areas (see drawing 3 on the facing page). For very bulky, nonfraying fabrics like Polarfleece, you may want to trim all structural seams to reduce bulk.

Trimming Darts

If your fabrics are heavy or bulky, also trim any darts. If a dart is ½ in. to ⅝ in. wide at the top, slash down the center of the fold, ending ¼ in. from the point. Make a small clip on one side so you can press the slashed area open, and press the remaining point to one side, as shown in drawing 4 on the facing page.

If a dart's top is wider than ⅝ in., trim it to ½ in. or ⅜ in. first, then slash it. You can slash smaller darts to within 1¼ in. of the point, then press open to distribute the bulk.

Grading

Enclosed seams, like those on collars, lapels, and cuffs, must be trimmed a bit differently than regular seams to reduce their bulk and allow them to lie flat with sharp, turned edges. To prevent a visible ridge on the garment's right side, trim the seam's two allowances to different widths, creating a gradual slope in the layered edges. Leave

Grade Enclosed Seams for Smoothness

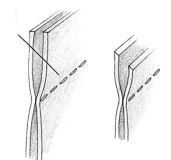

To reduce bulk and prevent ridges grade seam allowances by trimming to different widths, leaving the one next to the outside widest.

To grade a seam in one pass, make a beveled cut by holding shears at 30-degree angle to fabric, leaving edge farthest away from you wider than closer edge. This works best on thick fabric.

the top seam allowance (the one closest to the garment's right side) slightly wider than the one on the underside (see the drawing above).

Keep in mind that if you make a garment that has front facings with lapels, you'll need to clip the point where the roll line folds back at the front edge and reverse the grading order. Leave the facing's seam allowance widest above the clip, and the garment's seam allowance widest below the clip.

To grade a seam, trim the narrower side first, then trim the other side a little wider. You can also grade a seam by cutting both seam allowances at the same time, holding your shears at about a 30-degree angle to the fabric while cutting. This bevels the cut edges, and works best on thick fabrics (see the drawing above).

Cutting away part of your garment can be an intimidating step. But once you understand where to trim or grade and why this is so important, you'll be able to confidently use your scissors to achieve professional-looking seams. ■

Clip & Notch for Smooth Curves & Sharp Corners

Clip. Notch. These are likely to be scary terms when you're an inexperienced sewer, but clipping and notching are crucial for smooth, flat corners and curved seams—standard criteria for a garment of quality. Once you understand the difference between the two, and just how and when to clip or notch, you won't have any problem getting out your scissors and bravely tackling this step.

Scissors Savvy

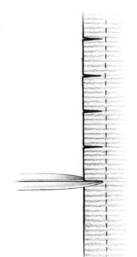

Use sharp, short-bladed scissors for the best control when clipping and notching, and position the blade carefully (left). For quick notching along curves, pink (below).

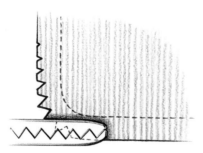

To avoid clipping the stitching line, hold scissors so tip of blade is at point where clip should end.

Use your pinking shears to make quick work of notching allowances on curved seams.

When to Clip, When to Notch

The word clipping refers to making snips into the seam allowance, perpendicular to the stitching line and $\frac{1}{8}$ in. to $\frac{1}{16}$ in. from it. Notching is done similarly along the seam allowance's edge, but it actually removes wedge-shaped pieces from the fabric. It is always best to staystitch the garment's edges at curves and corners before clipping or notching.

Clip concave (inside) curves where the distance of the cut edge measures less than the seamline. The clips let the seam allowance spread apart slightly so that it lies flat when the seam is pressed or turned. Clipping is also necessary on inside corners that will be turned or need to match up to a straight edge or an outside corner.

Notch convex (outside) curves where the cut edge is longer than the stitching line to reduce the outside edge and prevent bulky folds from forming when the seam allowance is turned and encased. Before you notch, fold the seam allowances over at the stitching line to see how much fullness needs to be removed for the allowance to lie flat. Notch the excess fabric where the folds form.

Clips or notches should be evenly spaced and made after seam allowances have been trimmed or graded. Place your clips and notches closer together on tighter curves.

Caveats for Scissors and Loosely Woven Fabrics

How you position your scissors is critical when clipping and notching seams. Hold them so that the tip of the blade is placed where you want the clip to end. Don't let the tip get any closer. And always be sure your scissors are sharp.

Try short-bladed scissors (like Gingher™ 4-in. embroidery scissors, available from Clotilde and Joanne's Creative Notions; see Resources on p. 87) for more control. If you hurriedly try to wing it with larger shears or dull blades, you may clip right through the stitching!

Handle loosely woven fabrics carefully when clipping or notching; if you get too close to the stitching, there's a chance the fabric will ravel. Staystitching, again, is helpful in preventing this. Another method is to make your clips no closer than ⅛ in. from the seamline.

Clipping and notching are very important steps for perfect curved seams and corners. So keep your scissors sharp and handy whenever you're sewing. Using them wisely will help you to get professional-looking results. ▪

Clip or Notch Curved Seams and Corners to Make Allowances Lie Flat

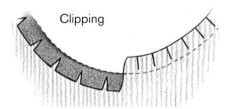

Clipping

Clip concave (inside) curve to within ⅛ in. to 1⁄16 in. of stitching so seam allowance's outer edge can spread when turned back.

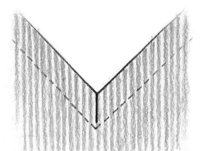

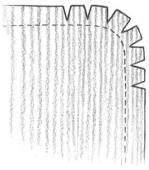

Clip inside corner so seam allowance can spread and lie flat when turned or can match straight edge.

Notch convex (outside) curve by clipping away V-shaped wedges from seam allowance to remove excess fabric.

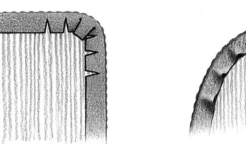

To determine where and how much to notch along convex curve, fold back seam allowance, then cut out excess fabric from the folds that will form.

Understitching

i f you've ever had a facing roll to a garment's right side, even when you've carefully pressed and tacked it down, you'll want to know about understitching—the technique of sewing the seam allowance to a facing or other layer. This trick is most commonly used to keep facings where they belong, but you can also use it on other garment sections that need extra help to stay in place, like under collars, welt pockets, and even lined patch pockets. Understitching is also a great way to keep

enclosed, narrow seam allowances flat when working with fabrics that don't press very well or can't be ironed with a warm iron.

Most fabrics can be understitched by machine using a straight stitch and a regular stitch length. But on fine, sheer fabrics, you may want to understitch by hand, taking very short regular running stitches. As with all techniques, it takes a little practice to do it properly, so let's take a look at how to understitch facings and then trickier areas, such as collars and pockets.

Grade and clip the seam before understitching (near right). Stitch with the facing right side up, using your fingers to help spread and "press" the facing as you sew (far right).

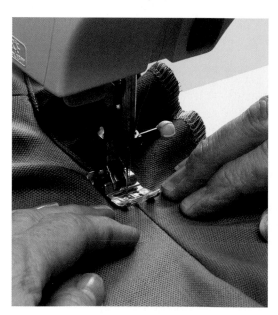

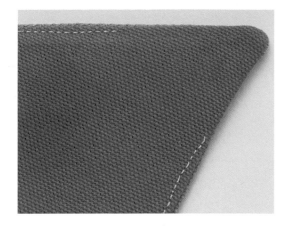

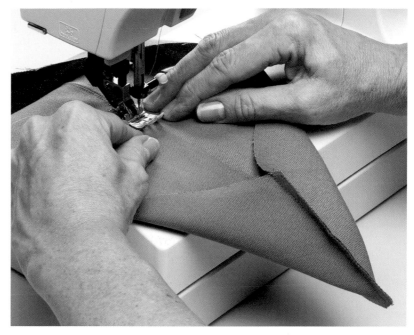

Understitch an under collar by beginning at the center of the long bottom edge, stitching toward the points as far as you can (right). Understitch short ends by beginning at the neck edge and stitching into the points (above).

To Understitch a Facing

First stitch the facing to the garment; then trim, grade, clip, or notch as necessary. Press the seam allowances toward the facing. Next, working from the facing's right side, edgestitch close to the seamline, catching both seam allowances (see the left photo on the facing page). It's important to keep the facing flat. Clipping around curved seams helps, but you also need to use your fingers as you stitch to spread the facing out, as shown in the right photo on the facing page. Don't stitch too tightly, letting the clips open up as you stitch. On some facings it's difficult, if not impossible, to edgestitch completely, but stitch as far as you can.

If you're understitching a front facing with a lapel, remember to stop stitching about ½ in. to 1 in. before the roll line intersects the front edge. Then turn your garment, and begin understitching from the other side to finish.

Understitching Hard-to-Reach Areas

When understitching under collars, it will be impossible to stitch all the way into the corners. Just stitch in as far as you can. You'll find that it's easier if you start from the center of the seam and work your way into a corner, going as far as you can by spreading the upper and under pieces apart (see the photo above right). This holds true for lined patch pockets as well. Understitch the long edges as far into the corner or curve as you can. Then draw the thread ends to the wrong side, and tie off securely at the beginning and end of your stitching so you don't have to backstitch, which adds bulk and may show through to the right side.

As you construct your garment, remember to understitch at each step, even if the pattern doesn't tell you to. The results are well worth the extra effort. You'll create a garment with smooth, flat seams that you'll be proud to wear. ∎

Flat-Felled Seams

Cover a rolled-hem/felled-seam intersection with a tiny appliquéd gusset.

Whenever you need a strong, narrow, self-finished seam for a one-layer garment, an elegant and easy choice is a flat-felled seam, such as you'll find at the side and underarm seams of a classic shirt and on the back of most blue jeans. In a flat-felled seam, one wide seam allowance is wrapped around a narrow one, then both are folded to one side of the seamline and top-stitched to one section of the garment.

The key to beautiful, easy felling is to use a specialized presser foot called a felling foot to ensure perfectly stitched and consistently narrow results. If you didn't get this foot with your machine, check with a dealer or try a mail-order source such as the Sewing Emporium (see Resources on p. 87).

The Foot Size Is Critical

A felling foot's size is equal to the width of the opening between the "toes" of the foot (or the width of the groove on the bottom, which is the same). This tells you not only how wide a finished seam that foot will make but also exactly how wide your seam allowances should be: One seam allowance should be the width of the foot, and the other should be twice that width, even if this seems ridiculously narrow.

For example, a 4-mm foot (common for European machines) will require one 4-mm (about ⅛-in.) seam allowance and one 8-mm seam allowance to make a 4-mm seam.

Rather than trying to trim ⅜-in. seam allowances to the right width later, you'll find it easier and more accurate to cut out seams using seam-allowance widths based on the foot right from the start.

Which seam allowance should be the wide one? The folded edge of a finished flat-felled seam with one stitching line showing will "point" toward the wider seam (see Step 2 on the facing page). It's a subtle difference, but it's usual to cut the back seams wider so the edge points to the rear.

Felling Takes Two Steps

Start by aligning the seamlines, not the raw edges, of your two layers, placing the wider seam allowance on the bottom. One side of a flat-felled seam has one visible stitching line; the other side has two. It's up to you which side you want to see. To show one stitching line, arrange your layers right sides together before sewing. For two visible lines, sew wrong sides together.

Fold and press (finger-pressing usually works fine) the extending portion of the wide seam allowance over the narrow one for approximately 1 in. at the start of the seam, as shown in the far left drawing on the facing page. Position the folded edge against the right inside edge of the foot and sew for about 1 in. without lifting the fabric into the foot. Then stop with the needle down and lift the folded raw edge over the horizontal blade at the front of the foot.

From here to the end of the seam, your job is to keep the two seamlines aligned. At the same time, you need to keep just enough of the wider, lower layer folded over so that it exactly fills the width of the foot as it slides over the blade and all three layers go under the foot. This step is easier if you just hold the layers, without having to worry about pulling out pins. If all goes well, both layers will be stitched on their seamlines, and the folded layer on top will be stitched right along its raw edge. Even if you occasionally miss the raw edge slightly, if the two layers stay correctly aligned, the final seam will be perfectly strong.

The second step is to spread open the garment layers with the seam allowances on top. Then fold the seam allowances to the left to conceal the raw edge, and send the seam back through the foot. This time, position the stitching line against the right inside edge of the foot and lift the folded edge over the blade. All you have to do as you complete the seam is keep the layers fully separated and the first stitching line snug against the big toe of the foot. This will ensure that the second line of stitching is perfectly parallel to the first.

Felling Sleeves

If you're felling an underarm seam or any other tubelike structure, you obviously can't separate the layers completely for the second step. If you have a free-arm machine, simply feed the tube onto the arm as you stitch. If not, you'll have to turn the tube inside out and gather the tube up and around the pressor foot as you stitch the seam.

Crossing Seams and Hems

When working with lightweight fabrics, it's usually no trouble to flat-fell one seam over another, as you would at the armhole seam of a classic shirt. You can often get the increased bulk through the foot by holding the seam both behind and in front of the foot and gently assisting it forward. Test a scrap first to be sure.

If your fabric proves too thick for the foot, the simplest solution is to stop about 1 in. short of the seam you need to cross and start the seam again on the other side. When the seam is finished, press the unstitched portion to match the seam on either side, and topstitch it with a regular foot.

You can use this same strategy with a rolled-hem foot that refuses to roll over an

Using a Felling Foot

Step 1

Start with folded edge against foot and all layers under foot. Fold and finger-press edge. Stitch about 1 in.

Stop, needle down, and lift raw edge over blade.

Step 2

Separate layers, press folded edge over seam, align first seam against foot, and lift folded edge over blade.

intersecting flat-felled seam. This will be an issue only when the hem is a smooth curve or straight edge that crosses the seamline instead of blending into it. Then you'll want to complete the felled seam first, rolling or folding it over the hem. This is the easiest, strongest way to deal with rolled-hem/felled-seam intersections, so redraw hemlines, if necessary, to make sure they're cut this way.

If you want a hem that curves into and out of each seamline, it's best to roll the hems first, up to the start of each seam, then fell the seams, ending as close as possible to the finished hems. At the intersection, you'll need to clip the seam allowance of the wider seam so it can fold in the opposite direction from its rolled position.

The classiest (and fussiest) way to cover the clip is with a small, hand-formed, machine-appliquéd gusset, as shown on the facing page. But an easier alternative is to choose a small, preset embroidery motif from those available on your machine, and use it to simultaneously cover the clip and reinforce the seam/hem join. ■

Pressing 101

Pressing is a surefire way to improve your sewing, regardless of your skill level. A few good pressing tools combined with basic techniques and a little time at an ironing board can give a professionally finished look to everything you sew.

Three Ways to Use Your Iron

Be aware of the different ways you can use your iron—pressing, ironing, and steaming—and learn which is best for what you're sewing and the type of fabric you're working with.

Pressing involves applying heat and pressure to fabric with the iron and lifting the iron away, continuing this up and down motion along the fabric. Pressing is used to flatten seams, set permanent creases, and apply fusible interfacings and stabilizers, for example, to all types of fabric.

In contrast to pressing's up-and-down movement, ironing involves sliding the iron back and forth directly on the fabric. Ironing is used to remove wrinkles.

Steaming—holding the iron above the surface of the fabric so the steam can penetrate—also relaxes wrinkles. But steaming is also used to mold and shape fabric. For example, before setting in a sleeve, you can steam the top of the sleeve cap to shrink it slightly, so it more easily conforms to the armhole.

Make It a Habit

Pressing should be a routine part of your sewing process. Press each seam and dart as you go, so it will lie flat and smooth before you stitch across it to join it with another seam. To set the stitches, press the seam or dart first through all layers as it was sewn. Then press it open, or to one side, as indicated by your pattern instructions. To prevent stretching or distorting the fabric, avoid using a circular motion and try to press in the direction of the lengthwise grain of the fabric. Set the press by allowing the fabric to cool thoroughly before you move it.

The action of pressing is different from ironing: Ironing slides along the fabric with a back-and-forth motion. To press, apply heat and pressure to fabric with the iron, lift the iron, and move on down the fabric.

Steaming relaxes wrinkles by penetrating the fabric with moisture and heat. To steam, hold the iron away from the fabric, then, to set the press, allow the fabric to completely dry before moving it.

A Seam Stick's half-round shape keeps it flat on the ironing surface and prevents the cut edges of the seam allowances from being pressed into the garment and leaving ridges on the right side.

Choosing an Iron

Irons come with many options, at many prices. But whichever type you choose, look for one that's comfortable to hold. Select a soleplate with a horseshoe-shaped hole pattern at the tip half, which gives a more powerful burst of steam, and a solid area at the back for faster drying of the steamed area. An iron with a stainless-steel soleplate resists scratching and sticky buildup from fabric finishes, spray starch, and fusible interfacing. And consider the convenience of an iron that operates with tap water. The new steam-generator ironing systems provide powerful steam from a base that holds the water, thus allowing the attached iron to be lighter weight than traditional irons.

Use a Stable Pressing Surface

If you use a standard ironing board, it should be a comfortable height (hip height is ideal) and stable enough to provide a firm pressing surface. Metal ironing boards should have sufficient holes to allow moisture to easily escape.

You can also make your own pressing table by padding and covering a large piece of plywood or an unfinished door and placing it on filing cabinets, a tabletop, or some other means of support.

An ironing pad should be made from wool or cotton, which absorbs moisture (¼ in. thick for ironing boards and ⅜ in. for pressing tables is ideal). Another choice is the new synthetic, hydrophobic pads, which wick moisture away from pressing surfaces so it can evaporate without being absorbed first. Use a 100 percent cotton cover for your ironing board or pressing table because cotton dissipates the heat evenly and allows moisture to evaporate.

More Tools for Perfect Pressing

There are many aids that can improve your pressing, but here are three of great value:

1. A press cloth, used to prevent shine or iron marks on fabrics that are sensitive to the heat of the iron. Try an 18-in. square of fabric, matched in weight to the fabric being pressed, using a lightweight cotton for lighter fabrics, like cotton, synthetics, silk, or blends, and a heavier cotton or wool for wools or thicker fabrics. Use the cloth dry or dampen it evenly with water to create steam when needed.

2. A pressing ham provides a surface that simulates the curves of the body and is used to press and shape darts, princess seams, collars, and other curved areas of a garment.

3. A hardwood Seam Stick, invented by Belva Barrick, of Glendale, AZ, (shown above right) makes pressing hard-to-get-at seams in sleeves and pant legs easy. It's useful for pressing all seams because its rounded top keeps seam allowance edges from getting pressed into the fabric and producing ridges on the right side of the garment.

Pressing takes just a little extra effort, but it can make a big difference in your finished results. So be sure your iron's always ready to go whenever you sew. ■

Utility Stitches

ost sewing machines made in the past 30 years have utility stitches that provide wonderful solutions to everyday sewing chores. These classic stitches were created to handle special fabrics and produce seams, hems, and other effects that can't be accomplished with the basic straight or zigzag stitch. Here's a brief refresher course on utility stitches and some ways they're used. The techniques represent some, but by no means all, of the things that can be done with the utility stitches found on most machines.

A Stitch by Any Name

Every machine brand uses its own names for stitches. If your stitches have different names or don't look exactly like those shown here, find the closest stitch your machine offers, which will probably produce the same results as those in the samples.

The roster of specialized utility stitches you'll find on most machines includes the following:

• The overlock stitch produces a stretchy seam and edge finish for knits, or an edge finish (but not a seam) for woven fabrics.

Utility Stitches for Special Seams

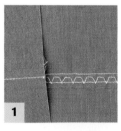

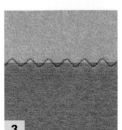
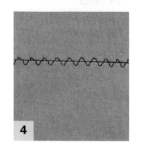

1. For a mock-felled seam, use the overlock stitch to finish the seam allowances (s.a.s). Sew the seam as called for in the pattern, trim the s.a. to ⅜ in., press the seam open, then press it to one side (double-pressing helps it lie flat). Sew the s.a.s together with the overlock stitch and press them to one side. Then, from the RS, straight-stitch ¼ in. from the seam.

2. For a very strong seam on heavyweight fabrics, like the crotch seam on denim, use the triple straight stitch. Don't use this stitch on a fabric weaker than the seam itself, because if something gives way under heavy use, it should be the seam, not the fabric.

3. For a decorative effect, or to reduce bulk in thick, nonraveling fabrics, make a strong fagoted seam with the running stitch: Butt two thick fabrics' edges together and stitch them centered under the needle.

4. Or for an open seam, press under the s.a. on each piece and stitch the two pieces together with a ¹⁄₁₆-in. gap between them.

- The running stitch produces a strong, wide stitch, which is both utilitarian and decorative, and can be used for fagoting seams, understitching, or applying elastic.

- The blind-hem stitch stitches forward, then zigzags once to the left. When a hem is folded, the tip of the zigzag catches a few threads of the fabric for a tiny hem-stitch.

- The super stretch stitch consists of very short, narrow zigzags alternating with slightly wider zigzags, which makes a strong, stretchy seam for medium- to heavyweight knits.

- The universal stitch alternates straight stitches on either side of a zigzag and is ideally suited to couching narrow elastic and cords.

- The triple straight stitch, is done by sewing forward four stitches, back two, then forward four again, eventually straight-stitching over the seamline three times. It produces a very strong seam.

- The double overlock stitch combines forward and reverse straight stitches with a zigzag, producing a smooth seam and edge finish for lightweight knits, and can also be used for couching.

Presser Foot Assistance

Many machines come with a selection of presser feet, like the overlock and the blind-hem foot, which are intended to assist you with guiding the fabric and the machine with forming the stitch. For the best results with utility stitches, use these and other feet suggested in your instruction manual.

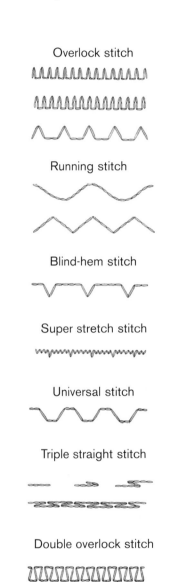

Utility Stitches

In addition to the basic straight and zigzag stitches, refer to your machine's instruction manual to find the same or similar stitches as those shown below. Then make samples to see how they work.

Overlock stitch

Running stitch

Blind-hem stitch

Super stretch stitch

Universal stitch

Triple straight stitch

Double overlock stitch

Make Samples for Reference

To practice the techniques shown here, make samples on 6-in.-square fabric scraps. Tinker with the stitch-length and -width adjustments to get the best results that you can. Keep the samples, along with their instructions, in plastic sleeves in a three-ring binder of tips and tricks. The samples provide a quick reference when you're trying to remember how something was done, and while making the samples, you'll probably think up more tricks of your own! ◼

Use the running stitch to attractively understitch a facing and help reduce bulk in heavy fabrics.

Utility Stitches for Knit Fabrics

1. Use the super stretch stitch in place of the straight stitch for seams on medium- to heavyweight knits. To prevent the fabric from stretching and creating a wavy edge, place a finger behind the presser foot to cause a minor "traffic jam" of fabric as it exits the presser foot.

2. Use the overlock stitch for seams in medium- to lightweight knits.

3. From Bernina instructor Millie Schwandt of Eugene, OR, comes a great variation on the technique shown in many machine manuals for applying lingerie elastic: Use the running stitch to sew the elastic, picot side down, to the nylon tricot on the RS, stretching the elastic as you sew, then turn the elastic to the tricot's WS and stitch again, stretching the elastic as you sew.

Make Quick Work of Hems and Facings

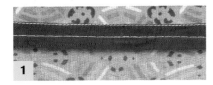

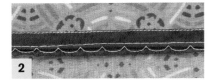

1. On knits and tightly woven fabrics, the blind-hem stitch alone can finish the raw edge and stitch the hem. Before hemming fabrics that might ravel, finish the raw edge with a fold or hem tape. Press the hem and machine-baste it in place ¼ in. from the raw edge.

2. Fold the hem to the RS along the basted line. Position the fold against the RS of the blind-hem foot's stitch guide, and adjust the blind-hem stitch width so that when the needle swings to the left for the zigzag, it just nicks the fold, catching only a few threads.

3. Remove the basting thread, unfold the hem, and press flat to finish.

Couch Heavy Thread with Utility Stitches for Various Gathered Effects

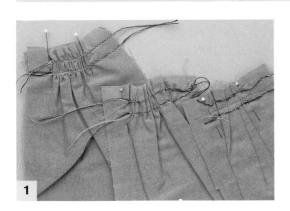

1. Couch two rows of heavy topstitching thread or lightweight cord with a zigzag or blind-hem stitch, draw up the topstitching thread, stitch down the gathers, and then remove the couching threads and cord. You can produce different effects with the gathers by varying the stitch length when couching. For a tightly gathered effect (left), use a very short zigzag stitch and a very loose needle-thread tension (so the couching threads can be removed easily). Lengthen the zigzag-stitch length to make softer gathers even though the amount of fabric gathered remains the same (center). For very loose gathers, couch the topstitching thread, catching it with the zigzag of a blind-hem stitch set at its longest stitch length. If you want to manipulate the gathers into pleats, make sure the zigzag stitches in each row are perfectly aligned with each other (right).

2. Create heavy elastic shirring by couching elastic cord with the double overlock stitch, being careful not to stretch the elastic cord. When all rows are couched, draw up the elastic cords. You can sew rows of couched elastic cord close together using a pintucking foot to guide the stitches.

3. Couch narrow elastic with the universal stitch set wide enough so that it doesn't catch the elastic, then draw up the elastic to create gathers.

Ripping Out Stitches

r ipping out stitches is never fun, but it's a necessary part of sewing. So here are some things you should know about the right tools and techniques for effectively ripping out straight, zigzag, blind-hem, stretch, and some serger stitches with a minimum of stress on your fabric and no trace of the unwanted stitches.

5

4

3

Tools to keep handy for ripping out stitches: conventional seam ripper with round or flat handle (1, 3), surgical seam ripper (4), curved manicure scissors (5), and flat-ended tweezers (2).

2

1

The tools to keep at hand are a conventional seam ripper, a surgical seam ripper, a pair of curved manicure scissors, flat-ended tweezers, and masking tape. A good conventional seam ripper should have a tiny, round, sharp point and a sharp inner curve (a safety ball is optional). A surgical seam ripper is indispensable for slicing through zigzag and serger stitches because its curved point is less likely than a conventional seam ripper to pierce the fabric. A pair of fine curved manicure scissors is useful for taking out complex stitches. Use the tweezers and/or the masking tape to remove loose threads.

After ripping out stitches, use an iron to press and steam the fabric carefully. This helps close needle holes and restore the grain of the fabric. Napped fabrics will benefit from a careful brushing as well as steaming.

Straight and Other Machine Stitches

To rip straight stitches, first carefully pick out the backstitching at both ends of the seam with a conventional ripper's sharp point. Then pick out the stitches. To remove the thread ends, smooth the sticky side of the masking tape over the seam, then lift it, pulling out the leftover thread bits. Or use the tweezers to pick out thread ends.

Remove zigzag stitches with a surgical seam ripper. First remove the backstitching at both ends of the seam, then pick out the stitches and remove the thread ends.

Ripping machine blind hems requires a combination of the straight and zigzag techniques. Reverse-action stretch stitches are not easy to remove because you need to cut each stitch. The repeat stitching pattern (for example, in triple straight stitches or mock overlock stitches) makes these seams very durable but resistant to quick ripping. Because these stitches are often used on knit fabrics, which can run if pierced, it's important to unpick with care.

Clip open each stitch on the top side of the seam with a very fine pair of nail scissors, turn the fabric over, and pull the bobbin thread loose. Use masking tape or tweezers to remove the clipped threads.

Ripping Serger Stitches

To rip out serger stitches, you'll need to combine the techniques for ripping straight and zigzag stitches. For a three- or four-thread overlock seam, work with a seam ripper on the top side of the seam, and cut through every fifth or sixth needle stitch, just as you would a conventional straight-stitched seam. Turn the fabric over, and gently pull the bottom needle threads away. The looper threads will come free at the same time. Use masking tape to remove stray threads. Rip two- or three-thread flatlock or two-thread overlock stitches in the same way as for machine zigzagging.

It isn't advisable to rip out a rolled hem because the fabric edge is likely to fray. Given the tiny dimensions of the hem, it's much easier and cleaner to just serge a new rolled edge, and trim off the old one in the process.

Ripping out stitches is an inevitable part of sewing, which will be much easier if you use these techniques. Remember that ripping out and correcting stitching mistakes can make the difference between a passable garment and a well-sewn one. ■

To Rip Out Machine Stitches

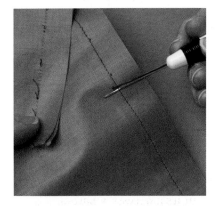

Straight Stitches

Use a conventional seam ripper for straight stitches. Pick out backstitching at both ends of seam with ripper's point. Working from top side of seam, slip seam ripper's point under every fifth or sixth stitch and cut. Turn fabric over, and use ripper's point to pick out 1 in. or so of bobbin thread. Lift bobbin thread, and pull away from fabric.

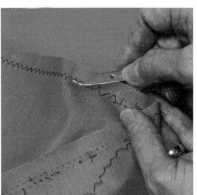

Zigzag Stitches

Use a surgical seam ripper to easily rip out zigzag stitches. Working on top side of seam, slide ripper through zigzags, cutting stitches' diagonal threads. Turn fabric over, and lift bobbin thread away.

Blind-Hem Stitches

Use a combination of techniques for straight and zigzag stitches: Gently pull hem away from garment. Using point of either conventional or surgical seam ripper, carefully clip through zigzag stitches holding hem in place. Remove straight stitches in hem allowance as for straight stitches.

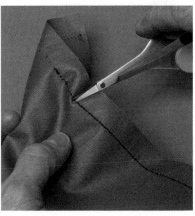

Reverse-Action Stretch Stitches

Clip open each stitch on top side of seam with very fine pair of nail scissors. Turn fabric over, and pull bobbin thread loose.

Fastening Threads

When you begin or end a row of machine stitching, you must fasten the threads to prevent stitches from unraveling. Here are some common methods and guidelines for securing threads on a machine.

Backtack—Also called a backstitch, a backtack is the most frequently used means of securing threads. Strong and quick to do, it works well on medium- to heavyweight fabrics to begin and end most stitched lines, except for dart points (ways to fasten threads on dart points are discussed below). A backtack is rarely used on soft or lightweight fabrics, since it adds stiffness and can distort the fabric. As well, seams in lightweight fabrics don't lie completely flat along the backtacked sections and are sometimes difficult to remove without damaging the fabric.

To backtack, begin by sewing forward ⅝ in., then stitch in reverse for two or three stitches. Sew forward to complete the stitching line, stopping ½ in. from the end, then sew in reverse for two or three stitches and then continue stitching to the raw edge.

Spot tack—A spot tack is used when stitching on the garment's right side because it's less conspicuous than a backtack. More appropriate for casualwear than for better garments, spot tacks are used to begin and end topstitching on patch pockets, collars, and cuffs.

To spot tack, set the stitch length to 0 (or drop the feed dogs), take two or three stitches in place, then adjust the stitch length for the seam (or raise the feed dogs), complete the line of stitching, and spot tack at the end. When speed-sewing, hold the fabric firmly so it doesn't feed under the needle for two or three stitches.

Short stitches—Used to secure the threads on fine garments and delicate fabrics, short stitches aren't as stiff or as difficult to unpick as a backtack, but they're also not as strong. Short stitches are frequently used on edges that will be faced, crossed by a hem, or trimmed, and are useful when joining bias strips.

Backtack

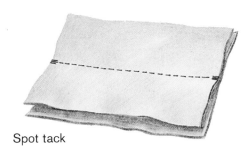

Spot tack

To secure threads with short stitches, set the stitch length to 1 mm and sew forward ¾ in., then reset the stitch for the seam and sew to ¾ in. from the end. Reset the stitch length to 1 mm and continue sewing to the edge.

Tailor's knot—The preferred method in haute couture, a tailor's knot is also used in casualwear to secure threads at dart points, tucks, and on lines of topstitching that end in the middle of a seam. Knots are time-consuming to make, but they're soft, neat, and easy to remove, and seams secured with knots lie flat when pressed open.

To secure threads with a tailor's knot, leave long thread tails at both ends of the stitching line and tie them together as one strand. If the stitching ends in the middle of a seam, pull the needle thread to the bobbin side, give both threads a sharp tug to remove any slack in the last few stitches, tie them in a tailor's knot, and trim the thread tails to ½ in.

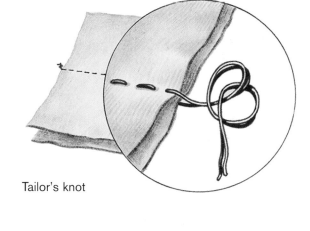

Tailor's knot

Bobbin stitching—Ideal for dart points and tucks on very sheer fabrics, bobbin stitching involves using a continuous strand of thread in the needle and bobbin. This method creates a soft, neat finish, but produces a weaker fastening than those sewn with two strands of thread.

Begin by threading the machine as usual, but leave the needle unthreaded. Pull out 15 in. of bobbin thread, insert this thread into the needle from the back, tie it to the needle thread, then wind the needle thread around its spool, pulling the bobbin thread up through the machine. Continue winding bobbin thread twice the length of the line to be stitched onto the spool. Begin stitching at the dart point, or tuck's end, and sew to the garment's edge. ■

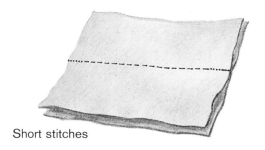

Short stitches

Sewing in a Zipper

Machine-baste the zipper tape to both seam allowances, stitching through the tape and seam allowance only (above). Draw a chalk guideline on the fabric ⅜ in. from the seamline and topstitch the zipper in place, starting at the bottom and stitching to the top on each side (right).

at one time or another, every sewer will probably need to insert a zipper into a garment. Regardless of the type of zipper—standard or invisible—or insertion method—centered or lapped—with a little bit of preparation, you'll be able to do it easily with great results.

Both standard and invisible zippers come in a variety of lengths. Start with a zipper that's slightly longer than the zipper opening on your garment, especially when working with a standard centered or lapped application—it's usually easier to shorten a zipper than it is to insert it precisely into a given space. For example, if your garment has a waistband, you can insert a longer-than-needed zipper that extends beyond the waistline seam, stitch over the zipper, and trim away the excess when you attach the waistband. You can cut a zipper at the bottom to shorten it as well; just be sure to add a new zipper stop by whipstitching over the teeth at the bottom of the zipper, then cutting it ½ in. to 1 in. below this new stop.

Interface the Zipper Area

Before inserting a zipper, it's a good idea to add a strip of interfacing along the seam allowance, especially when using a lightweight or unstable fabric, to help support the zipper's weight and stabilize the fabric. Use a strip of lightweight, fusible interfacing that's about 1 in. wide and the length of the zipper opening. Fuse the interfacing strip to the zipper-opening seam allowances, extending over the seamline about ⅜ in. For a crisp opening edge, interface only the seam allowances.

The Centered Zipper

Sew the garment seam, machine-baste the zipper opening's seam allowances together, and press the seam open. One side at a time machine-baste the zipper tape to each seam allowance, then topstitch the zipper in place from the right side of the garment. For best results, and to avoid rippled edges, topstitch directionally from bottom to top on each side through all thicknesses. Use your

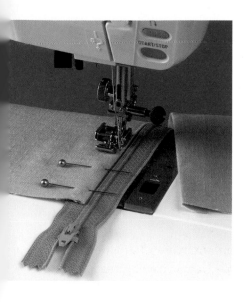

Pin and stitch the right side of the zipper opening to the zipper tape, with the fold near the zipper teeth and the stitching close to the fold (far left). To make the lap on a lapped zipper, adjust the remaining seam allowance to ½ in. and pin in place, covering the zipper teeth and the first row of stitching (near left).

machine's zipper foot, which allows you to stitch close to the zipper teeth, and remove the seamline basting stitches once the zipper is inserted.

The Lapped Zipper

Sew the garment seam, and baste the zipper opening seam allowances together. Lightly press them open, and then remove the basting stitches. Keep the zipper closed, and pin the right side of the opening to the zipper, placing the fabric fold close to the zipper teeth. Using a zipper foot, stitch close to the fold through all thicknesses. To create the lap, refold the seam allowance on the left side, making it ½ in., and pin to the zipper tape, just covering the zipper teeth and the previous stitching line. Lightly chalk a line about ⅜ in. from the lap fold to use as a top-stitching guide (be sure this line clears the zipper teeth and catches in the left seam allowance). Then topstitch the zipper in place from bottom to top.

The Invisible Zipper

This is the easiest and fastest zipper application, because there's no need to baste or top-stitch. Use an invisible zipper foot of the same brand as the zipper. This lets you sew extremely close to the zipper coils, making them invisible from the right side.

Always insert this zipper before sewing the garment seam. First unzip the zipper and press the coils as flat as possible with a cool iron, as shown in the top right photo above, and don't close the zipper again until after inserting it.

Positioning this zipper might be confusing at first. Just remember to always keep the zipper and the garment right sides together with the zipper coils along the seamlines. And position the zipper foot for each side of the zipper so the needle clears the center hole and the coils glide under the groove.

Sew the left side of the zipper to the right garment section, top to bottom, until you get to the zipper stop. Align the remaining tape to the left side of the garment and sew in place. Then complete the garment seam.

Keep in mind that you cannot stitch the seam so it connects smoothly to the zipper stitching without leaving a gap. Start the seam as close to the zipper stop as possible, then hand-sew the gap closed. Or machine-stitch the seam completely, but switch to a zipper foot to get those final stitches as close to the stop as possible. ■

Before inserting an invisible zipper, press the zipper's coils as flat as possible with a cool iron (top right). Stitch down each side of the invisible zipper with coils along the seamline, right sides of zipper tape and fabric together (above). Stitch as far as the zipper stop will allow you to stitch.

Darts Build Shape into a Garment

a dart is a long tuck that narrows to a point at one or both ends to build shape into a flat piece of fabric. Darts are extremely important for fit and style. It's easy to achieve perfect darts that shape the bust, hips, waist, and back of a garment, provided you remember to mark accurately, stitch carefully, and press gently.

Well-fitting darts should point to, and end slightly before, the fullest part of the body. To check for placement and fit, pin-fit the pattern before cutting your fabric by pinning it along the darts and seamlines. Then "try it on" to check the position, length, and shape of the darts (see p. 16).

Darts can be straight, concave in shape (with legs that curve inward), or convex (with outward-curving legs). If you need to add room in the dart area of your garment, a concave dart takes up less fabric and adds needed fullness; conversely, a convex dart removes excess fullness for a closer fit. Making a dart slightly longer or shorter may also be necessary to match your body's shape (see the drawings on the facing page).

Transfer Darts Accurately from Pattern to Fabric

Mark darts with tracing paper, marking pencil, or tailor's tacks made with thread or pins. Tracing paper and marking pencils should be used on the fabric's wrong side only, and avoided on sheer fabrics since they can leave permanent marks on the right side. When using a tracing wheel, use a ruler as a guide to trace the lines of a straight dart and a French curve as a guide for curved darts.

If you use a marking pencil, cut the garment piece and, before removing the pattern tissue, stick a pin through the pattern and both layers of fabric at each dot along the dart. Lift the pattern piece and place a small mark on the wrong side of each layer of fabric at the point where the pin comes through.

For tailor's tacks, the procedure is similar, but marks are made with thread or pins rather than with a pencil. For thread tacks, see p. 20.

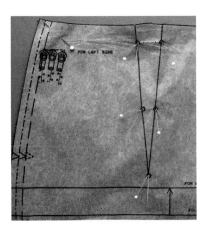 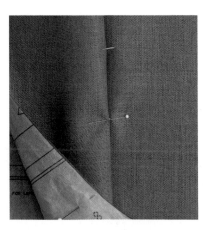

Tailor's tacks made with pins transfer darts accurately and quickly, without leaving permanent marks: Insert a small-headed pin through the pattern and fabric layers at each dot on the dart; flip to the other side and insert another pin at each pinned point. Gently pull the fabric layers apart, slipping each pin back through the fabric to mark each dot, and finish separating the layers.

Pin tacks require a little practice, but they're accurate and fast and won't leave permanent marks on your fabric. To learn how to make pin tacks, see the photos on the facing page.

Stitching Perfect Darts

Use ¼-in.-wide masking tape as a guide to stitch curved or straight darts that are well tapered at the point (see the photo above, left). Be sure to remove the tape as soon as the dart is completed so that the adhesive doesn't remain on the fabric.

When stitching an open-ended dart at a seam or edge, begin at the wide end, backstitching at the seamline, then stitch to the point and off the fold. Don't backstitch at the point; rather, leave long thread ends and tie them together in a tailor's knot (see p. 71). To stitch a double-ended dart, sew from the middle of the dart to one point. Then flip the garment to the other side so you can again sew from mid-dart to the other end, overlapping the stitches in the middle, leaving long thread ends, and knotting at each point.

If you're sewing darts in sheer fabrics, or when darts are sewn on the right side of a garment for a design detail, you can eliminate the thread knot at the dart end by stitching with one continuous thread. To do this, pull your bobbin thread up through the needle plate and thread it through the needle from back to front (the reverse of normal threading). Then continue to thread the

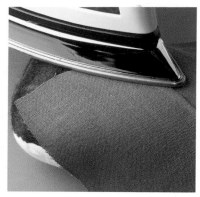

machine in reverse to the thread spool and wind enough of the bobbin thread around the spool to stitch the dart. Then stitch the dart from the point to the wide area.

Pressing Darts Is Critical

Press stitched darts first on each side, just to the end of the dart, so you don't crease your fabric beyond the dart point. Then press to one side as indicated in your pattern over a tailor's ham to retain the curved shape. To prevent the dart's outline from showing on the right side, insert a piece of heavy paper between the dart and the garment while pressing. Turn the garment to the right side and press again, checking to make sure the point blends smoothly into the rest of the garment. Use a press cloth, if your fabric requires it, when pressing from the right side. Follow these steps and you'll have the beautiful, smooth darts that are so important to the fit and look of your garment. ■

Use ¼-in. masking tape as a stitching guide. Sew the dart from its wide end to and through the point. After removing the tape, press the stitched dart over a tailor's ham.

Altering a Dart's Shape

You can alter a dart's shape and length to better fit an individual body. To add room in the dart area, curve the dart legs inward to make a concave dart and/or shorten the dart. To remove excess fullness, make the dart convex and/or lengthen it.

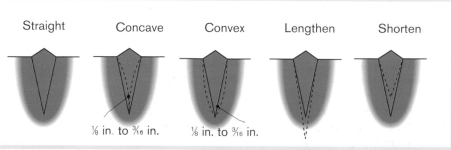

Straight Concave Convex Lengthen Shorten

⅛ in. to ³⁄₁₆ in.   ⅛ in. to ³⁄₁₆ in.

Pleats

Pleats add a distinctive design element to any garment, but their main function is to provide fullness or ease within that garment. Here's a description of the various types of pleats and how to form them. Also included are some things to think about when choosing fabrics for pleated garments.

A Glossary of Common Pleats

All pleats involve folding the fabric, and each folding strategy produces a different type of pleat. A box pleat has two folds that are folded away from the front of the fabric, and the inside folds may or may not meet at center. A box pleat is most commonly used as a single pleat—for example, at the back of a shirt yoke.

An inverted pleat also has two folds, but they're folded toward the front of the fabric,

making it a box pleat turned inside out. Like a box pleat, an inverted pleat is commonly used as a single pleat.

You can also make an inverted pleat with a separate underlay, using a matching or contrasting fabric to form the underlay. This type of pleat can be tricky to hem. You can hem the garment and underlay separately before sewing them together. Or you can hem after joining the underlay: Clip the seam allowances just above the hemline, and press the seam allowances in the hem toward the underlay and away from the underlay above the hemline.

Knife pleats are really the simplest of all pleats because they consist of a series of single folds, all in the same direction. Knife pleats are always used in multiples, whether continuously around a garment or in small groups.

A continuous set of very narrow (⅜ in. to ½ in.) knife pleats are called accordion pleats. And sunray pleats refer to a continuous set of narrow knife pleats that are narrower at the top and usually worked on fabric cut on the bias. Both types of these narrow pleats are dimensional and stand away from the body when worn. Because they're so narrow, they're best created by commercial pleating companies or formed on home pleating machines (see Resources on p. 87). But all of the other pleat types are easy to form in your garments if you follow a few simple steps.

Partially top- or edgestitch pleats to keep them flat, if pressing isn't enough. Stitch through all garment layers.

Forming Pleats

It's important to first carefully mark the pleat's fold and placement lines on the wrong side of the fabric with chalk; transfer to the right side with thread basting. When making box pleats, it's easier to mark and form inverted pleats on the garment's wrong side, which then become box pleats on the right side.

Form the pleats by folding along each foldline and bringing it to the placement line. Baste through all the layers, then press in place. To keep pleats flat and close to the body near the waist, top- or edgestitch them in place for several inches.

To keep the pleats' edges crisp along their length, edgestitch along the outside or inside pleat folds through the pleat layers only if pressing doesn't do the job. When edgestitching, try to stitch from the bottom up to maintain the direction of the grain and prevent rippling. Or try a solution of vinegar and water spritzed on the edge of the pleat before pressing to establish a crisp edge (one-third vinegar to two-thirds water should do it, but for more power, make it half and half).

Fabric Considerations

When choosing fabrics for pleated garments, the fabric's ability to hold a crisp crease is something that you need to consider. And keep in mind the fabric's weight as well.

Because getting a sharp edge on a pleat involves pressing with a hot iron, natural fiber fabrics are the best if you want a really crisp finish. Synthetics and knits that won't take the iron's heat are best left as soft-edge pleats. Lightweight fabrics in natural fibers are the best choice for most types and widths of pleat. If you want to pleat heavier fabrics, use wider pleats to prevent bulk at the seamline that joins them to the waistband or other garment sections.

Remember that most pressed pleats will come out with washing. The best way to

Types of Common Pleats

Box Pleat
Two equal fabric folds are folded away from front of fabric. Folds can, but need not, meet at center.

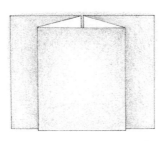

Inverted Pleat
Two equal folds of fabric are folded toward front of fabric.

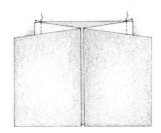

Inverted Pleat with Separate Underlay
Separate piece of fabric forms back of pleat.

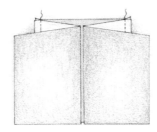

Knife, or Side, Pleats
Continuous set of pleats folded to one side.

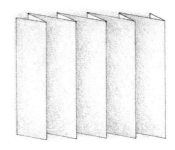

Accordion Pleats
Continuous set of very narrow knife pleats.

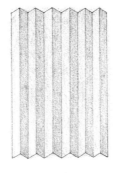

Sunray Pleats
These narrow knife pleats are wider at top and usually worked in bias-cut fabric.

Mark Pleats Carefully

Use a chalk marker to make fold and placement lines on WS; then transfer with thread basting to RS.

Knife Pleats

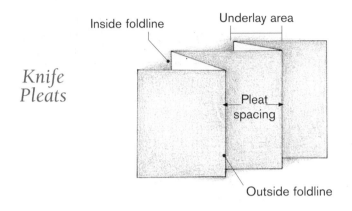

Inside foldline

Underlay area

Pleat spacing

Outside foldline

Box Pleat

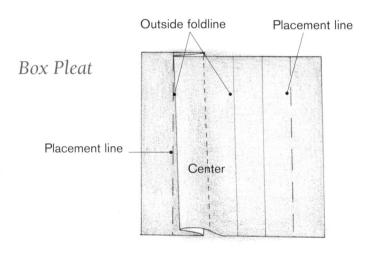

Outside foldline

Placement line

Placement line

Center

Inverted Pleat

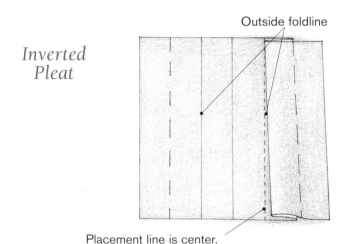

Outside foldline

Placement line is center.

permanently set pleats is to have it done by a commercial pleating company (see Resources on p. 87). According to the San Francisco Pleating Co., it's strictly fiber content that determines whether a pleat is permanent. Only synthetics will stay pleated after washing, so permanent pleating usually requires at least 50 percent synthetic fiber. Then hand washing and line drying is recommended.

If you're not using a pattern that calls for pleats, carefully calculate your yardage requirements. Measure the distance for each pleat from foldline to placement line plus the amount for pleat spacing. Multiply this by the number of pleats you plan. When using a commercial pleater, the yardage requirements depend on the type of pleat, but the general rule is three times the yardage called for. In other words, 3 yd. will pleat down to 1 yd.

You can use pleats in a lot of different ways, so give them a try in your next project. They take a little time, but pleats are an easy way to add interest, as well as room, to your garments. ■

Hemming Separate Underlay

To eliminate bulk in hem of pleat with separate underlay, clip seam allowances above hem edge. Press toward underlay in hem and away from underlay in pleat.

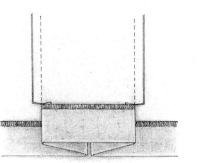

Great Gathering— A Sure Thing

a t one time or another, most sewers have had to gather a large area of fabric into a smaller area to add fullness to a garment or other project in an area like a sleeve, skirt, or ruffle. Many discover that, at first, the procedure is not as simple as it sounds. By following a few guidelines, you can avoid frustration and achieve beautiful results.

Gathering Options

The type of project you're sewing will determine the best method of gathering to use, whether it's a casual garment, home decorating project, or fine-quality garment. The options include sewing a zigzag stitch over a cord (for example, for curtains), stitching over transparent elastic (for casual garments), and—the most challenging way but with the best results—sewing several rows of straight stitching (for better garments).

Tips for Fine Gathering

The goal in gathering is to create small, even folds in the fabric that are evenly distributed along the gathered area. Check your pattern guide sheet for all the areas to be gathered—sewing all of them at the same time will speed up your work.

Gather across seams or not—

If your fabric is lightweight, sew the gathering after the cross seams are stitched, the edges finished, and the seams pressed open. But, if the fabric is medium- to heavyweight, gather each section separately from stitching line to stitching line, and then assemble the adjacent sections.

How full should gathers be?—

The ratio of flat area to gathers is often determined by your pattern, but there are general guidelines you can follow. A 2:1 or 2½:1 ratio gives an attractive amount of fullness in most fabrics. This means that 40 in. to 50 in. of fabric would be gathered into a 20-in. length. The fabric density (thickness), the hand (soft or crisp), and the length of the gathered area affect how full the gathering

Joining Gathered and Flat Areas

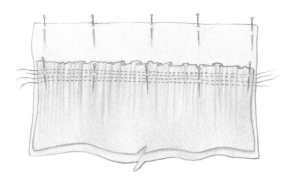

Divide edge to be gathered and edge it will be attached to into equal number of divisions. Pull bobbin threads to gather, and match marks to prepare for stitching.

Handling Seams

Lightweight Fabric

Medium-to-Heavy Fabric

For lightweight fabrics, gather across seam allowance (left). For medium- and heavyweight fabrics, break gathering rows at stitching line (right).

can be, or how much fabric can be coaxed into a given area. An extreme example of gathering was done on pleated Fortuny skirts of fine georgette, where a 6½:1 ratio was used with great results. In these skirts, 180 in. of fabric was first pleated, then gathered onto a 28-in. waistband.

The Gathering Rows Are Key

For fine gathering, machine-stitch two, three, or four parallel rows of stitching ⅛ in. apart, then pull the bobbin threads to gather the fabric to length. Four rows of stitching give the most control and the best results.

Stitch length— The ideal stitch length for gathering depends on the fabric and the ratio of gathers to flat fabric, but it can vary from four to ten stitches per inch. For a light- to medium-weight fabric, try starting with 8 sts/in.

Each machine stitch forms a knot in the fabric, which takes up space when the bobbin thread is pulled and the knots move close together. The stitches must be short enough to make small, even folds, yet long enough for the gathers to fit into the required area. The shorter the stitch, the more control you have over the gathers; the longer the stitch, the more fabric you can fit into a small area.

Adjust bobbin thread and tension— Since the bobbin thread is the one you'll pull to draw up the gathers, a different-color, stronger thread (topstitching thread, for instance) used in the bobbin will be easier to see and less likely to break. A slightly looser upper tension, or tighter bobbin tension, makes it easier to slide the fabric to be gathered along the thread. The tension must be tight enough so the fabric rides snugly on the thread, but loose enough that you can pull the thread without breaking. When you use a heavier thread in the bobbin, you automatically cause the bobbin tension to tighten, so you don't need to adjust it.

Mark divisions for matching— To make it easier to gather evenly, divide into an equal number of sections (whether fourths, eighths, or sixteenths) both the edge to which the gathered edge will be joined and the edge to be gathered. Mark the divisions on each side with thread tracing, marking pencil, or pins, as shown in the drawing on p. 79. The smaller the sections, the more control you have when adjusting the gathers.

Sew the lines for gathering—Stitch the first gathering row slightly inside the seamline, on the garment side, and the remaining rows in the seam allowance. Don't backstitch, and remember to leave long tails for pulling. If your machine has an adjustable needle position, sew the first row by moving the needle slightly to the left of center, then follow the throatplate guideline for the required seam allowance. For the next row, adjust the needle position so you're stitching ⅛ in. to the right of the first row; repeat for the desired number of rows.

Pulling up the gathers—Match up the marks and pin the two sections together, taking care not to pierce the gathering stitches. Starting at one end, pull all bobbin threads together, pulling up half the area to be gathered until it's slightly smaller than half the area to which it will be attached. Avoid pulling both the upper and bobbin threads—the stitching will lock and require removal. Pull the bobbin threads on the other end in the same way, and wrap the threads in a figure eight around a pin on each end to temporarily secure the gathers.

Working on a padded surface like an ironing board, pin the fabric taut and adjust the gathers evenly between pins. A seam ripper or an awl helps distribute the gathers. Tighten the bobbin threads, if needed, then pin the layers at even intervals, or hand-baste if the fabric is slippery.

Stitch the Gathered Seam

To join the gathered and flat edges, change the bobbin thread and stitch the seam with the gathered area on top. You'll stitch between two rows of gathering, as shown in the drawing below. Hold the fabric on each side of the presser foot so the gathers lie at right angles to the seam, adjusting any unevenness and removing pins as you come to them.

After sewing the seam, remove the row of gathering thread that shows on the right side of the garment, and tie the ends of the other rows of stitching separately. Press the gathers in the seam allowance with the tip of an iron, being careful not to flatten the gathers below the seamline. Finish the seam as desired and press in the direction it should lie in the garment.

Staying a Gathered Seam

If you plan to join a gathered area to a bias edge of fabric, you'll need to add a stay to the bias side first to stabilize the length. A lightweight stay made of rayon seam tape or the selvage from china silk or rayon lining works well. Baste the stay to the wrong side of the bias area so it will be included in the seam, then attach the gathered side. ■

Ready to Stitch

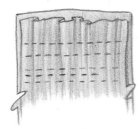

Stitch between first and second rows of gathering stitches. Later, remove first gathering row.

Bias Strips Made Easy

regardless of the type of sewing you do, at one time or another you're likely to need strips of fabric for binding, trimming, or otherwise finishing an edge. Strips used for binding edges, especially curved edges (as well as strips used for trims), should be cut on the bias because fabric cut on the bias has some stretch and hence shapes well around curves. Bias strips have the advantage of not

raveling along the edges. These strips are usually cut on the true bias, which is the exact 45-degree diagonal of a fabric's straight grain, while the bias grain is any diagonal line across the fabric

There are several ways to cut bias strips. Three are shown here, a fourth is on p. 85.

Cutting Bias Strips

Quick Home-Dec Method

STEP 1. Fold a piece of fabric, RS together, to be a square. Sew around three open sides. Cut off corners to get scissors blade inside. Press seams open, and trim to ¼ in.

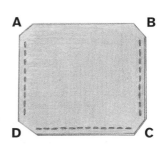

STEP 2. Cut one layer from A to C, then cut other layer from B to D.

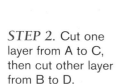

STEP 3. Lay resulting tube on table and cut strips of desired width for three-quarters length of tube.

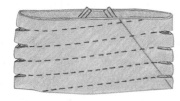

STEP 4. Refold tube so uncut area is on top. Draw line connecting first cut on one side to second cut on other side. Repeat for all cuts. Cut along lines.

Cutting Bias Strips

With a Rotary Cutter

STEP 1. Establish fabric's true bias by straightening fabric's grain, measuring equal distances from one corner along both selvage and crossgrain, and connecting end points.

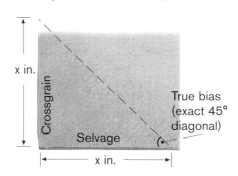

STEP 2. Use rotary cutter and clear ruler to cut bias strips of desired width.

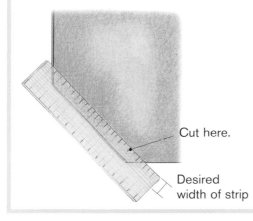

Cut here.

Desired width of strip

From a Perfect Square

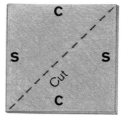

C = Crossgrain
S = Straight grain

STEP 1. Cut fabric into perfect square, then cut on diagonal.

STEP 2. Mark strips on one triangle, join both triangles along straight-grain edges, and extend strip marks onto second triangle.

STEP 3. Join opposite crossgrain edges offset by one strip width, and cut, following marked lines.

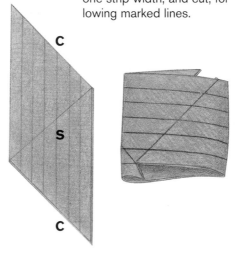

Join and Trim Bias Strips

STEP 1. Trim ends of strips square, then place RSs together at right angles and mark diagonal at corner along fabric's straight grain. Sew, using very short stitches (1mm). Don't backstitch.

STEP 2. Press seam open, then trim seam allowance to ¼ in.

Taper.

STEP 3. Taper seam edges to reduce bulk.

The best method for your project depends on your equipment, the length of the strip you need, and whether or not the placement of the seams that join the bias strips is important to the project. For the rotary-cutter method, you'll also need a cutting mat and a transparent ruler to cut one strip at a time. This method gives you some choice over the length of each strip, so that when joining the strips, you can position the joins as desired along the edge being bound. To join strips cut this way, follow the instructions in the drawings above.

Cutting a continuous strip from a perfect square is a quick and accurate way to create bias strips (see drawing above). This method works well on medium-weight, fairly stable fabrics but produces strips with seams not evenly placed along the strip.

The third and fastest method, shown in the drawings on the facing page, is borrowed from the home-dec industry, where quantities of strips are often needed. This technique eliminates wasted fabric but, like the second method, results in unevenly spaced seams. ■

Perfect Piping

To inconspicuously join piping in a seam, butt the cording's ends, then overlap the ends of the fabric, with the top layer folded under ¼ in. Whipstitch the cording together, then blind-hem the fabric in place.

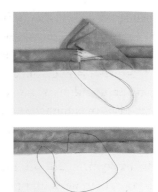

To calculate the fabric width needed to adequately cover cording, wrap the cording with a scrap of fabric, clip at the seam allowance, and unwrap and measure the distance between clips.

To sew the bias-cut strips of fabric around the cording, use a zipper foot and stitch close to the cording.

t he next time you want to add a great finishing detail to a garment consider the decorative possibilities of piping. You can use piping almost anywhere—all you need is a seam. Piping is a versatile and decorative detail to use in seams or along the edges of garments, pillows, and other home furnishings. In addition to being decorative, piping can provide added strength along a seamline and create a smooth transition between connecting sections. Although piping technically refers to a folded, flat trim inserted in a seam, the term is more commonly used to describe covered cording sewn in a seam. You can buy piping ready-made, but fabric choices are limited, so here's how to make your own and apply it to garments and other projects.

Covering the Cording

First choose a cording that's compatible with your fabric and project. You'll find several types and sizes, ranging from soft cable cord

To ease the piping around curves and corners, clip or notch the piping's seam allowance. Notch to remove excess fabric on inside curves (1); clip to spread the fabric on outside curves (2); and for square corners (3), sew to the corner point, stop with the needle down, and make one clip to the stitching line. With thicker cording, it may be necessary to take one or two diagonal stitches to turn the corner.

to firm drapery-pull cord, which are available in the notions or decorating departments of most fabric stores.

Cover the cording with fabric strips cut on the bias rather than on the straight grain—bias-cut fabric molds smoothly around the cord and is more flexible when rounding curves and corners. You can cut the strips using any of the methods explained on p. 82, p. 83, or p. 85. To determine how wide each fabric strip should be to adequately cover the cording and allow enough fabric to extend into the seam allowance, wrap the cord with a fabric scrap and pin it in place. Use a hem gauge or small ruler to mark the amount of seam allowance, clipping through both layers, as shown in

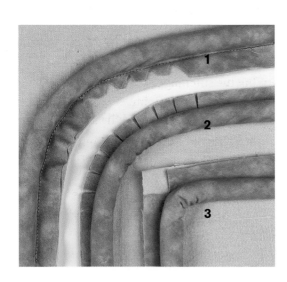

the top left photo on the facing page. Unwrap and measure between the clips to find the exact width of fabric needed.

To make piping, fold a bias-cut fabric strip around the cording, right side out with cut edges matching. Use a zipper foot and stitch slightly away from the cord to hold the fabric in place (see the bottom left photo on the facing page). Leaving this bit of slack ensures that the holding stitches won't show when the piping is sewn to the garment. Try not to stretch the strips lengthwise as you stitch because they become narrower when stretched.

Sewing the piping to your garment is a two-step process. First sew it to one garment section, then attach the adjoining section, right sides together, sandwiching the piping in between. Stitch through all of the fabric layers with the zipper foot snug against the cording.

Starting and Joining Ends

If piping is inserted in a single straight seam, the ends will be sewn into an adjoining seam. But if the piping is to completely encircle a pillow, for example, or the outer edge of a jacket, you'll need to join the ends together.

The best way to create an inconspicuous join is to overlap the ends of the piping. Start the piping on a long edge, not at a corner point (if there is one), and begin the stitching about 2 in. from the end of the piping. Sew completely around the item, ending the stitching about 2 in. from where you began. Cut the piping, leaving a 1-in. overlap. Remove enough of the stitches from the fabric covering the overlapping end of the piping so you can turn the fabric under ¼ in., trim the cording so the ends meet, and hand-stitch the cord and fabric ends respectively in place (see the top right photos on the facing page). Then sew the joined piping section to the item.

Continuous Bias

Make a continuous strip of bias, and save time by stitching one long seam instead of several short seams to connect the individual strips.

Start with ½ yd. of fabric and trim off ends as shown.

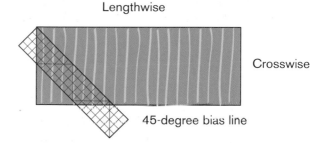

Lengthwise

Crosswise

45-degree bias line

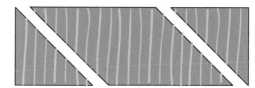

Mark strips and cut, using rotary cutter, leaving 1-in. uncut borders on top and bottom.

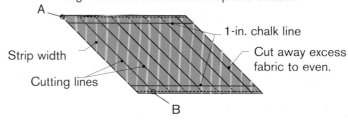

A

1-in. chalk line

Strip width

Cut away excess fabric to even.

Cutting lines

B

Stitch long ends, RSs together, with ¼-in. seam, matching A to B. Press seam open and cut strips apart with scissors.

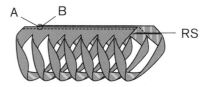

A   B

RS

Corners and Curves

The trick to well-piped corners and curves is to shorten the stitch length as you sew them, and clip or notch the seam allowances as appropriate (see the bottom right photo on the facing page). ■

Contributors

Susan Andriks

Choose the Correct Pattern Size, p. 12
Susan Andriks is the owner of The Fabricsmith, a studio specializing in bridal and special-occasion clothing. A sewing teacher and writer, she is the author of *Bridal Gowns: How to Make the Wedding Dress of Your Dreams* (Palmer & Pletsch).

Jan Bones

Pattern Layouts, p. 24
Cutting Out, p. 28
Staystitching, p. 46
Sew a Perfect Seam from Beginning to End, p. 48
Directional Sewing, p. 52
Jan Bones designs lingerie patterns for her company Lingerie Secrets. She is the author of *Lingerie Secrets: Sew a Perfect Fit for Every Body* (Krause Publications) and has produced a number of sewing videos.

David Page Coffin

Easing in a Seam, p. 50
Flat-Felled Seams, p. 60
David Page Coffin is an associate editor of *Threads*.

Barbara Emodi

Must-Have Tools, p. 42
Ripping Out Stitches, p. 68
Barbara Emodi has taught sewing classes in the United States, Canada, and Australia. A freelance writer from Canada, she has written extensively for *Threads* magazine and other publications.

Joanne Molesky

Trimming and Grading Seams, p. 54
Clip & Notch for Smooth Curves & Sharp Corners, p. 56
Understitching, p. 58
Joanne Molesky is freelance technical writer in Canada where she has taught sewing classes and developed pattern instructions.

Karen Morris

Bias Strips Made Easy, p. 82
A contributing editor of *Threads* magazine, Karen Morris works as a freelance writer and designer. She is the author of *Sewing Lingerie that Fits* (The Taunton Press) and has designed her own line of hand-loomed knitwear.

Celeste Percy

A Trip to the Fabric Store, p. 6
Making a Duplicate Pattern, p. 14
Sewing in a Zipper, p. 72
Pleats, p. 76
Perfect Piping, p. 84
Celeste Percy is a writer and teacher of sewing and fiber arts-related classes. She is the owner and teacher of the Sew Happy Studio, a sewing school for children and teens in Eugene, OR.

Mary Roehr

Pressing 101, p. 62
Mary Roehr, of Sedona, AZ, writes and teaches classes on tailoring and pressing.

Claire Schaeffer

Fastening Threads, p. 70
Claire Shaeffer, a writer and teacher from Palm Springs, CA, is the author of *Couture Sewing Techniques* (The Taunton Press).

Shirley L. Smith

Tissue- and Pin-Fitting, p. 16
With-Nap Layout Basics, p. 26
Darts Build Shape into a Garment, p. 74
Great Gathering—A Sure Thing, p. 79
Shirley L. Smith teaches sewing and is the author of *The Art of Sewing: Basics and Beyond*, available from her at The Sewing Arts (PO Box 61418, Denver, CO 80220; (303) 321-8037). She is a member of the National Sewing Guild and The Fashion Group International.

Millie Schwandt

The Secrets of Machine Needles, p. 36
Construction Threads, p. 40
Millie Schwandt teaches sewing classes at 27th Street Fabrics in Eugene, OR, including all the Bernina machine, serger, embroidery, and software classes as well as free-motion machine embroidery, heirloom sewing, and serger construction classes.

Toni Toomey

Making Your Mark, p. 19
Straight Pins, p. 34
Presser Feet, p. 38
Utility Stitches, p. 64
Toni Toomey has been sewing for 40 years and contributes articles to *Threads* magazine.

Resources

Clotilde

B3000
Louisiana, MO 63363
(800) 772-2891
www.clotilde.com
Do-Sew Tracing Paper, home pleating machines, invisible zipper foot, marking tools and materials, Omnigrid™ rulers, pattern paper, portable cutting tables, ripping tools, Roll-a-Pattern, rotary supplies, scissors, sewing notions, and tools, Weight Mates

A Great Notion Sewing Supply

101-5630 Landmark Way
Surrey, BC V3S 7H1
Canada
(800) 309-2829
Marking tools and materials

Joanne's Creative Notions Plus

PO Box 44030
Brampton, ON, L6V 4H5
Canada
(800) 811-6611
www.joannescreativenotions.com
Home pleating machines, marking tools and materials, Omnigrid rulers, pattern paper, pinpoint tracing wheel, ripping tools, Roll-a-Pattern rotary supplies, scissors, Sewer's Fix-it Tape, sewing notions and tools, special-order cutting tables, Weight Mates

Koppel Pleating

890 Garrison Ave.
Bronx, NY 10474
(718) 893-1500
Professional pleating company

M&M Ladies' Belt and Pleating

614 Alexander St.
Vancouver, BC V6A 1C9
Canada
(604) 255-7921
Professional pleating company

Nygard International

1771 Inkster Blvd.
Winnipeg, MB R2X 1R3
Canada
(204) 982-5034
nygard.com
Professional pleating company

Nancy's Notions

333 Beichl Ave.
Beaver Dam, WI 53916
(800) 833-0690
www.nancysnotions.com
Marking tools and materials, Omnigrid rulers, pattern paper, Pellon TruGrid®, pinpoint tracing wheel, portable cutting tables, ripping tools, Roll-a-Pattern, rotary supplies, Sewer's Fix-it Tape, sewing notions and tools

San Francisco Pleating Co.

425 2nd St.
San Francisco, CA 94107
(415) 982-3003
Professional pleating company

Sewing Emporium

1079 Third Ave.
Chula Vista, CA 92010
(619) 420-3490
Specialized presser feet, including felling feet

Simplicity Pattern Company

Consumer Relations Dept.
901 Wayne St.
Niles, MI 49121
(888) 588-2700
Burda's Tracing Set; Grid tissue paper

Credits

The articles compiled in this book appeared in the following issues of *Threads*.

p. 6: "A Trip to the Fabric Store" by Celeste Percy, issue 87. Photos © Sloan Howard.

p. 9: "Grainline", issue 60. Illustrations by Robert LaPointe.

p. 12: "Choose the Correct Pattern Size" by Susan Andriks, issue 86. Photos © Sloan Howard. Illustrations by Karen Meyer.

p. 14: "Making a Duplicate Pattern" by Celeste Percy, issue 88. Photos © Sloan Howard.

p. 16: "Tissue- and Pin-Fitting" by Shirley L. Smith, issue 65. Illustrations by Carla Ruzicka.

p. 19: "Making Your Mark" by Toni Toomey, issue 66. Illustrations by Robert LaPointe

p. 22: "Shrink before You Sew" issue 61. Illustrations by Michael Dinges.

p. 24: "Pattern Layouts" by Jan Bones, issue 81. Illustrations by Christine Erikson.

p. 26: "With-Nap Layout Basics" by Shirley L. Smith, issue 74. Photos © Sloan Howard. Illustrations by Kim Jaeckel.

p. 28: "Cutting Out" by Jan Bones, issue 85. Photos by David Page Coffin, © The Taunton Press, Inc.

p. 30: "Preventive Sewing-Machine Maintenance" by Sally Hickerson, issue 91. Photos by David Page Coffin, © The Taunton Press, Inc.

p. 34: "Straight Pins" by Toni Toomey, issue 71. Photos by Scott Phillips, © The Taunton Press, Inc. Illustrations by Carla Ruzicka.

p. 36: "The Secrets of Machine Needles" by Millie Schwandt, issue 68. Illustrations by Frank Habbas.

p. 38: "Presser Feet" by Toni Toomey, issue 73. Illustrations by Michael Gellatly.

p. 40: "Construction Threads" by Millie Schwandt, issue 70. Photos by Scott Phillips, © The Taunton Press, Inc.

p. 42: "Must-Have Tools" by Barbara Emodi, issue 92. Photos © Sloan Howard.

p. 46: "Staystitching" by Jan Bones, issue 77. Photos by Scott Phillips, © The Taunton Press, Inc.

p. 48: "Sew a Perfect Seam from Beginning to End" by Jan Bones, issue 76. Photos by Scott Phillips, © The Taunton Press, Inc.

p. 50: "Easing in a Seam" by David Page Coffin, issue 72. Illustrations by Kathy Bray.

p. 52: "Directional Sewing" by Jan Bones, issue 94. Photos © Sloan Howard.

p. 54: "Trimming and Grading Seams" by Joanne Molesky, issue 78. Illustrations by Kathy Bray.

p. 56: "Clip & Notch for Smooth Curves & Sharp Corners" by Joanne Molesky, issue 80. Illustrations by Michael Gellatly.

p. 58: "Understitching" by Joanne Molesky, issue 82. Photos by Scott Phillips, © The Taunton Press, Inc.

p. 60: "Flat-Felled Seams" by David Page Coffin, issue 64. Illustrations by Michael Gellatly.

p. 62: "Pressing 101" by Mary Roehr, issue 95. Photos by Chris Timmons, © The Taunton Press, Inc.; photo on p. 63 © Belva Barrick.

p. 64: "Utility Stitches" by Toni Toomey, issue 75. Photos by Scott Phillips, © The Taunton Press, Inc. Illustrations by Christine Erikson.

p. 68: "Ripping Out Stitches" by Barbara Emodi, issue 83. Photos © Sloan Howard.

p. 70: "Fastening Threads" by Claire Shaeffer, issue 67. Illustrations by Michael Gellatly.

p. 72: "Sewing in a Zipper" by Celeste Percy, issue 89. Photos © Sloan Howard.

p. 74: "Darts Build Shape into a Garment" by Shirley L. Smith, issue 79. Photos © Sloan Howard. Illustrations by Karen Meyer.

p. 76: "Pleats" by Celeste Percy, issue 84. Photos by David Page Coffin, © The Taunton Press, Inc. Illustrations by Kathy Bray.

p. 79: "Great Gathering—A Sure Thing" by Shirley L. Smith, issue 63. Illustrations by Robert LaPointe.

p. 82: "Bias Strips Made Easy" by Karen Morris, issue 69. Illustrations by Carla Ruzicka.

p. 84: "Perfect Piping" by Celeste Percy, issue 90. Photos © Sloan Howard.

Front matter photo credits

p. iii: Scott Phillips, © The Taunton Press, Inc.
pp. v, vi, 1: © Sloan Howard

Section openers photo/illustration credits
p. 5: Michael Dinges
p. 33: Scott Phillips, © The Taunton Press, Inc.
p. 45: © Sloan Howard

Index